Automotive Technicians

Helen Ginger

ISBN 978-1-934302-43-9

TSTC Publishing
Texas State Technical College Waco
3801 Campus Drive
Waco, Texas 76705

http://publishing.tstc.edu/

Publisher: Mark Long
Project manager: Grace Arsiaga
Copyediting and proofreading: Kayla Allen
Printing production: Bill Evridge
Indexing: Michelle Graye, indexing@yahoo.com
Graphics specialist: Stacie Buterbaugh
Editorial intern: Cori Weyhe

Manufactured in the United States of America

First edition

Table of Contents

Commonly Used Abbreviations

AAS	Associate of Applied Science
ACC	Austin Community College
ASA	Automotive Service Association
ASE	(National Institute for) Automotive Service Excellence (Certification)
AUT	Automotive Technician
ATRA	Automatic Transmission Rebuilders Association
AYES	Automotive Youth Educational Systems
BSME	Bachelor of Science in Mechanical Engineering
CAP	Chrysler College Automotive Program
ELITE	Mercedes-Benz Enthusiasm, Loyalty, Integrity, Talent, Excellence
L1	Advanced Engine Performance Specialist Test
MDT	Master Diagnostic Technician
NATEF	National Automotive Technicians Education Foundation
OES	Occupational Employment Statistics
OOH	Occupational Outlook Handbook
PACT	Honda Professional Automotive Career Training
STC	GM Service Technical College
STEP	BMW Service Technician Education Program
TSTC	Texas State Technical College
T-TEN	Toyota Technical Education Network

UTI   Universal Technical Institute
VOTEC Vermilion Occupational Technical
        Education Center

Chapter 1: Automotive Technician Careers

Most technicians choose the automotive field because they love working on cars. Many grew up helping dads or uncles work on cars and trucks in their driveways or in shops. Some enjoy helping people or like the job stability of being an auto technician. Some choose it for the money. In today's world of technologically advanced cars, an automotive tech can have a successful, long-term career and make a comfortable living.

Turn on the television and it won't be long before a dealer or manufacturer ad for a car or truck flashes across the screen. Drive down the highway and count the vehicles you pass or, in the case of traffic, the number that pass you. It doesn't take long to be reminded of America's ongoing love of cars and the constant redesign, retooling, reshaping and, perhaps most importantly, reconfiguration of the "brains" of today's automobiles. The expanding complexity of automotive technology results in an ever growing demand for trained technicians. Recent Bureau of Labor statistics project that by 2016 at least 883,000 automotive service technicians and mechanics will be employed – an increase of 110,000 since 2006.

The twenty-first century Automotive technician (AUT) must be more than good with his or her hands. AUTs must be adept at analyzing problems. They have to study technical manuals and use mathematical skills. Strong communication and computer skills both come into play on a daily basis. Many older working auto techs remember when cars were simple and the first excursion to the moon was an event of great complexity. Today's graduating

AUTs will work on cars containing more computers than lifted off with the first spaceship.

The world has come a long way in a short time. Today's trained automotive technicians can expect rewarding careers in a technical field with almost unlimited possibilities and specializations.

AUT Overview

In 1860, a Frenchman named Etienne Lenoir patented the first practical gas engine in Paris and, in 1862, drove a car based on the design from Paris to Joinville. Siegfried Marcus, of Mecklenburg, built a car in 1868 and showed one at the Vienna Exhibition of 1873. His later car, called the Strassenwagen, had about 3/4 horse power at 500 rpm. It ran on crude wooden wheels with iron rims and stopped by pressing wooden blocks against the iron rims. It had a clutch, a differential and a magneto ignition. Karl Friedrich Benz, owner of a small mechanics shop, is generally accepted to be the inventor of the first true gasoline automobile. Built in 1885-86, his three-wheeled, four-stroke, engine and chassis automobile was powered by an internal combustion engine. Not long after his vehicle came the Curved Dash Oldsmobile with a single cylinder engine, tiller steering and chain drive. It sold for $650. In 1901, 600 were sold.

From Paris to Vienna to Mannheim to Detroit, what do these early cars have in common with the vehicles of today?

The people who work on them.

Passenger cars, trucks, buses, motorcycles, tractors and race cars could neither be built nor repaired without automotive technicians. Modern society depends on its vehicles. Vehicles depend on AUTs.

The first vehicles, although astounding for their time, were simplistic when compared to today's cars. Modern-day automotive technicians have to know and understand electrical systems, drive trains, engine cooling systems, automatic transmissions and transaxles. Hollywood still tends to depict auto mechanics as grease-covered guys in dirty overalls. Today's reality for an automotive technician is far different.

Both men and women work in the field – a field that tends to be more "surgical" than greasy. While the AUTs of today do work on brakes and clutches, they also work on microprocessors, in-board computers, electronic fuel-injection systems, integrated global positioning systems, as well as automobiles and trucks powered by electricity and other fuels such as ethanol. The world is changing quickly and the new generation of AUTs is keeping up through education, diagnostic and problem-solving skills, and knowledge of electronics and mathematics that complement their mechanical aptitude.

These skills are perfectly suited to the automotive techs entering the field. They've grown up on the computer and the Internet. Some can break down an entire computer and rebuild it, the same way an AUT may check the components of a vehicle under repair. Using and understanding a global positioning system is not rocket science, but rather an everyday tool in the modern car for most AUTs enrolled in an Associate Degree program in Automotive Technology.

Working in the service field is not all pristine, though. Automotive technicians also lubricate engines and other components. They repair parts – or replace them before they break down. They solve puzzles, such as determining the exact cause of a malfunction. They maintain records of each job, listing everything they do and use. As part of their work day, they may use power tools, such as lathes and grinding machines, pneumatic wrenches, jacks and hoists, engine analyzers and welding equipment. While employers furnish the expensive equipment, AUTs acquire a collection of their own tools, such as screwdrivers, wrenches and pliers. That list of tools grows in relation to the number of years the AUT spends in the workforce.

Perhaps the most used tool of all is the automotive tech's diagnostic senses. AUTs take what they've learned in the classroom and on the job and apply it to their work. During schooling, they do more than learn theories. They work in the lab on real cars and trucks. They tear down, inspect, repair and rebuild. They develop the skills and senses to diagnose and solve problems.

When they graduate and leave the classroom they are far ahead of other techs without that training – in experience, knowledge, confidence and, ultimately, pay.

Employment Outlook

The employment outlook for automotive technicians is good. If the economy is doing well, people buy cars which will need maintenance. If the economy is slow, people keep their cars and those cars will need servicing and upkeep. Either way, automotive technicians are needed. The online site ELearning Yellow Pages states that "changes in economic conditions generally have minor effects on the automotive service and repair business."

According to the Occupational Outlook Handbook (OOH), "Automotive service technicians and mechanics held about 773,000 jobs in 2006. Automotive repair and maintenance shops and automotive dealers employed the majority of these workers -- twenty-nine percent each. In addition, automotive parts, accessories and tire stores employed seven percent of automotive service technicians. Others worked in gasoline stations; general merchandise stores; automotive equipment rental and leasing companies; Federal, State, and local governments; and other organizations. Almost seventeen percent of service technicians were self-employed, more than twice the proportion for all installation, maintenance and repair occupations."

Even better news is that the OOH predicts employment of AUTs to grow by fourteen percent by 2016.

As older techs retire, younger techs will take their place. Older AUTs leaving the workforce means that employers will be losing not just bodies but experience, so they will be looking for younger techs with training. Techs who have completed automotive training programs and have earned their

Automotive Service Excellence (ASE) certification will be in the highest demand. ELearning Yellow Pages says, "For well-prepared persons with a technical background, an automotive service technician career offers an excellent opportunity for good pay and the satisfaction of highly skilled work with vehicles incorporating the latest in advanced technology. However, people without formal automotive training are likely to face stiff competition for entry-level jobs."

The OOH agrees: "Some employers report difficulty in finding workers with the right skills. People with good diagnostic and problem-solving abilities, and training in basic electronics and computer courses are expected to have the best opportunities. Those without formal automotive training are likely to face competition for entry-level jobs."

Today's automotive repair field offers a wide array of positions, from automotive service technicians to parts specialists to service managers, in small independent shops or in huge dealerships.

O*Net Online reports that by 2016, there will be 26,540 job openings for automotive service technicians and mechanics due to growth and net replacement.

For those interested in a challenging, hands-on, evolving position, the career of automotive technician has a promising outlook.

AUT Employer Profile: Sam Sepulveda

After being a supervisor in 2006, Sam Sepulveda became the Fleet Manager overseeing the Rio Grande Valley sector. His job now puts him in charge of almost 2,000 vehicles (of the U.S. Border Patrol), from 1,550 line watch vehicles that are on constant patrol to special purpose vehicles, like ATVs and heavy equipment. He keeps track of the budget, oversees the garages and consults with the Washington headquarters for the Border Patrol. On his own, he's working to set up partnerships with schools teaching Automotive Technology.

"We are short-handed with techs. For those 1,550 line watch operation vehicles, we have right now a total of twenty-eight mechanics. We have three lead techs and six supervisors. We have, throughout the sector, a total of seven garages, are working on our eighth, and every garage is responsible for the repair of a certain number of vehicles for each station. So, basically, we're short right now by twenty to twenty-five mechanics. To my understanding the national industry ratio of vehicles to mechanics is like thirty-five to one."

Sepulveda envisions a partnership where AUT students would work twenty hours, thus getting the most use out of the hands-on time to learn the trade. He says the Border Patrol would be looking for all around mechanics: "My biggest advice to the young individuals who want to get into the automotive industry is to learn all the aspects of the vehicle." When he hires a tech, he looks at more than just which program the tech graduated from. "I look at academic grades. At the same time, you go back and see how much information you can get from the school, the instructor, about the individual. It comes down to determining how dedicated this individual is, how he did in school academically, was he absent a lot or not. All those things weigh strongly. In an agency, garage or dealership, it's all about production. We always try to keep an average of ninety-two to ninety-three percent of the fleet operational at all times."

Sepulveda also recommends that techs get their ASE certification: "ASE certifications play a very important role when it comes to showing your experience, knowledge and training. You want to make sure you put those certifications down on your resume because that puts you at a higher grade, a higher scale, when working for the United States government."

Sepulveda loves his job and plans on retiring with the Border Patrol. "We mechanics are the doctors for vehicles, so it's very important that we take our profession, our job, to heart and be very proud. Just as there's a lot of need for teachers and doctors, there's a lot of need for mechanics."

Salary Ranges

Not only can people entering the automotive technician field expect steady work, they can expect above average wages. According to the Occupational Employment Statistics (OES) for May 2007, the median hourly wage earnings of automotive service technicians and mechanics was $16.43, with the lowest ten percent earning less than $9.25 and the highest ten percent earning more than $27.72 per hour.

The average annual wages range from a low of $19,240 to a high of $57,650, with the median annual wage at $34,170.

Percentile	10%	25%	50% (Median)	75%	90%
Hourly Wage	$9.25	$12.14	$16.43	$21.92	$27.72
Annual Wage	$19,240	$25,250	$34,170	$45,600	$57,650

One Texas metropolitan area boasts the fifth highest concentration of AUT workers in the nation: Killeen-Temple-Fort Hood has an hourly mean wage of $17.72 and an annual mean wage of $36,850.

Overall, Texas beats the average national wages for automotive service technicians and mechanics. The hourly mean wage in Texas for AUTs is $16.77, while the annual mean wage is $34,880.

Area: Texas		
Period: May 2007		
Occupation (SOC code)	**Hourly mean wage**	**Annual mean wage**
Automotive Service Technicians and Mechanics	$16.77	$34,880

The Occupational Outlook Handbook says, "Many

experienced technicians employed by automobile dealers and independent repair shops receive a commission related to the labor cost charged to the customer. Under this system, weekly earnings depend on the amount of work completed. Employers frequently guarantee commissioned technicians a minimum weekly salary."

Considering this, it's important to note that automobile dealers are the second highest in median annual earnings for service technicians, just behind local governments. These figures are for all those in the automotive technician and mechanics field, regardless of prior education. Students graduating with an Associate of Applied Science degree in Automotive Technology enter the field with equivalent experience and a leg up on those without a degree.

Regional & Average Dealership Salary Figures		
Salary Figures by Position		
Position	Total US	West South Central (Includes Arkansas, Louisiana, Oklahoma, & Texas)
Master Technician	$68,128	$68,568
Mid-Level Technician	$43,479	$44,631
Entry-Level Technician	$28,122	$27,436
NADA, 2008		

All of these figures mean that the national average salary for AUTs is good and Texas' average salary for AUTs is even better.

AUT Student Profile: Ross Cruz

Russ Cruz says his passion has always been cars, but his life took a circuitous route to get to where he is today -- finishing his associate degree in Automotive Technology at Austin Community College (ACC). "I come from a family where everybody goes to school, goes to college and becomes a professional. I worked for Dell for a little over eight years, and before that I was a supervisor at an Avis. Then I went back to my passion, automobiles."

Cruz pulls from his experience at Dell. For one thing, he knows computers, which he feels play a major role in today's vehicles. "The days of the shade tree mechanic are kind of gone. Technology is where it's at now." Some of the things he's bringing from Dell to his schoolwork and job hunting are team work, networking and leadership skills. "Step up to the plate and help someone else out. You learn more and understand what you know and what you're doing. People look to me as the go-to person. I'm glad to be in that role. I also talk to the Department Chair here at ACC, let him know where I want to be and what I want to do. By networking, I hope to find others who can lead me in the right direction."

Currently, Cruz goes to school during the day. "Lately, I've tried to come in on the weekends to see if one of the lab technicians has something going on, just to gain a little more experience. I think any kind of job I can do just increases my knowledge and experience base. A good example -- I helped one of the lab techs out with replacing struts on a Highlander. A week after that, we did that segment in class. I knew exactly what was going on because I actually had my hands-on before reading about it."

With graduation soon, Cruz looks to the future. "One thing I definitely made sure before I left Dell was to keep in contact with a lot of managers because you just never know when I might need a reference. I also sat down with a shop owner and had a one-on-one with him, just to see what it was like. Another thing I did was send the Department Chair my resume and my career program, not for the next five years but just for now until graduation. I wanted him to know exactly who I am and it wasn't going to be just lip service. I wanted him to know I was a person who's really focused on doing this thing and to show him my credentials." Cruz takes advantage of his classroom time to ask questions. "I like to ask real world questions like salary. I ask: What's it like being out there? What's a typical day for you?"

Cruz is in the generic program at ACC, but is considering applying with a Toyota dealership. "There are other paths, too. I could work at a few different places just to get more experience. And then apply to Toyota by the time I have a pretty good track record with those managers and shop owners."

"I remember growing up and watching *American Graffiti* and seeing how the kids back in those days were so excited about cars. Our nation is so great because we're the only nation out there that grew up with cars. It's part of our mystique. Even when I check out Web sites in Japan where they have motorcycles and cars, they all want the muscle car or they all want the Harley-Davidson. It's just a mystique about our great nation."

Career Paths

Automotive Service Technicians have a wide range of career paths they can follow, especially those graduating from a formal training program such as a post-secondary vocational school or community college. Students in a post-secondary automotive technician training program receive intensive career preparation through classroom instruction and hands-on training and can earn their ASE certificates and, in the case of community college work, their associate degree. An associate degree often includes classes in customer service and other skills that can advance an AUT's opportunities for employment.

The Occupational Outlook Handbook 2006 strongly recommends that people seeking work in automotive service complete a formal training program. As a graduate of a post-secondary program, an AUT often has had hands-on instruction in reading manuals, working with electronics and maintaining records. An AUT with an associate degree will go into a career already holding ASE certification in one or more of eight different areas of automotive service. Graduates of post-secondary schools may decide to continue their education at four-year universities or may go directly into the workforce. Having skills in multiple areas of expertise, workplace experience and a proven work ethic, these technicians increase not only their value to employers, but their pay.

With a foundation built upon a post-secondary education, an AUT can move into various career fields, from working in large shops or multi-million dollar dealerships with specializations in electrical systems, engine repair, brake systems, engine performance, suspension and steering, heating and air-conditioning, automatic transmissions and transaxles, tune-up, manual drive train and axles to working in or owning smaller specialty shops or full-service independent shops.

Some formal education programs at community colleges offer certification in specific makes of vehicles. Texas State Technical College (TSTC) Waco has partnered with Toyota to offer the Toyota Technical Education Network (T-TEN) program, which provides product-specific training, and with Chrysler for a specialization called Chrysler College Automotive Program (CAP). In addition, TSTC has an advisory committee consisiting of members from within the business and industry. Other schools also offer training in specific makes of vehicles. With product specific training, an Automotive Technology graduate is ready to move into a dealership or independent specialty shop. This type of partnership and specialization, as well as determining whether the school offers certification by the National Automotive Technicians Education Foundation (NATEF) and whether its instructors are certified by ASE, is something prospective students should consider when choosing a community college.

Upon completion of a post-secondary program, an AUT can choose from many options -- working in a general automotive shop or gasoline stations; specializing in a particular area of expertise at a large shop or dealership; working in a specialty shop, automotive equipment rental and leasing companies, and general merchandise stores; joining Federal, State and local governments; or working toward management in any of those choices. In addition to working on specific makes of cars or on particular parts or systems of vehicles, there are also various positions available within the workforce, such as service adviser, service consultant, auto parts specialist, parts sales, diesel service technicians, small engine mechanics, heavy line technicians or many other choices. With this many options available, graduates find there are almost unlimited positions, salaries and growth potential available to them.

Job Titles

In the past, those working in the automotive repair field were called mechanics or even grease monkeys. In today's world, neither of those words represent the reality of the men and women who work on cars, buses, tractors, trucks, motorcycles, planes and more.

The most common title now is Automotive Technician or AUT. Today's AUTs work on complex machinery that includes more than gas engines and oil filters. They know automotive microprocessors, electronic fuel injectors and on-board diagnostic computers.

Graduation from a post-secondary program is not the end of training. It is the beginning of a life-time of learning. Completion of an automotive training program may be substituted for one year of experience, so that a graduating student not only has a degree or certification, the AUT usually enters the workforce with experience built in.

Over years, as the AUT works in the field, he or she moves from an entry-level technician to a mid-level tech.

If that tech specializes, the job title may change or evolve. Some targeted titles may be: Repair Service Estimator, Emissions Analyst and Repair Technician, Specialty Shop Technician, Shop Manager, Aftermarket Parts Research and Development, Parts Manager, and many others, depending on the specialization. Larger repair shops often employ specialized techs in areas like air conditioning, front-end, transmissions and heavy-line mechanics, drivability/emissions and radiator.

Even the title Automotive Technician is only a starting, generalized term. An AUT can become certified by ASE in eight different areas of automotive service. Once the tech is certified in all eight areas, he or she is then called a Master Automobile Technician.

Although specialized job titles may change over the years or with the job, the title of Master Automobile Technician stays with the tech and is one highly valued by both the tech and the employer.

AUT Working Tech Profile: Ray Hitchcock

Master Technician Ray Hitchcock started working on cars when he was ten years old. "My grandfather showed me how and my uncle had a shop. As a kid, I would spend the summer sweeping floors at his place and working on cars. My grandfather one time pulled a transmission out of his truck and set it on a table, then said, 'Here, take this apart and put it back together and it better work.' I was thirteen." While Hitchcock admits he didn't get it back together, he's quick to say he tried.

During his senior year in high school, he worked at a dealership as a porter. "Porters help the technicians out, change oil and run customers. I worked there for a year and finished high school mid-term. I went straight to Texas A&M, played baseball there, then decided to go back to turning wrenches. My best friend had a friend who had a shop and he was looking for somebody, so I started working with him and, after five years, ended up being half-owner."

After that shop closed, Hitchcock began working for Mobile Car Care in Houston, which eventually became America's Service Station. He was soon promoted to "starter." When a new store opens, the starter goes and literally starts the store. He's opened seven stores in Houston and has started both Austin facilities.

Hitchcock has been certified since 1986 and with his high school work he was able to claim two years of automotive experience. "I've been Master certified four times now. I've got twenty-two years professionally -- twenty-five altogether." He'll soon be going for his fifth Master's certification.

If students are trying to decide between a generic or a dealership-sponsored program, Hitchcock advises looking into the future. "If they plan on staying in the dealership and sticking with that dealership, I would go for the specialized program." Hitchcock has worked at both dealerships and independents. "I started out at a dealership and I've worked at a few more since then. But I like the independents more. You see different cars and there are fewer corporate hassles."

Whichever you choose, keeping your training current is important. "I went through training and classes. I did a couple at Austin Community College, went to the Ford training center at Texas A&M, did the field training center at San Jac. As a member of the Automotive Service Association (ASA), I'd get their notices and fliers of upcoming classes. I'd sign up and take them. Learning is a process. You have to update your training. It's part of your job."

Job Duties

Automotive Technicians analyze, diagnose, service and/or repair automobiles and light trucks that run on gasoline, electricity or alternative fuels such as ethanol. Servicing today's highly sophisticated vehicles requires both mental and physical skills. AUTs use computerized shop equipment and electronic components, as well as traditional hand tools. They practice shop safety and focus on hazardous materials control. They learn professionalism. Those with problem-solving abilities, good diagnostic skills and training in basic electronics and computer courses will move ahead in their careers.

Because today's automobiles have integrated electronic systems and complex computers, AUTs are called upon to have broad knowledge of how those complex components interact. At the same time, they must be able to read and decipher digital manuals and reference materials.

When an automobile comes into a shop with either mechanical or electrical troubles, technicians use a diagnostic approach to decipher the problem. They test to see if components or systems are working properly. They isolate the cause of the problem. If needed, they test drive the vehicle or use testing equipment to determine if the problem can be fixed or if a new component is required.

During routine service inspections, technicians test, repair or replace, following a checklist as they work. Finding and replacing or repairing worn parts can prevent future damage to the vehicle.

AUTs keep up with the latest manufacturers' service information and technical service bulletins. This is much easier today than it was twenty years ago since most shops receive automatic updates via the Internet or from software packages. They become familiar with equipment and instruments, such as digital volt ohm meters, digital storage oscilloscopes, brake lathes, computerized four-wheel alignment systems and graphing digital multimeters.

Most new cars now have automotive systems, like braking, transmission and steering, that are controlled primarily by computers and electronic components. Technicians have to be familiar with these advanced systems, as well as integrated global positioning systems, Internet access and alternative fuel systems.

An AUT's duties become more narrow as he or she specializes. Specializations can be as varied and as numerous as there are systems on a car: brake repairers, automotive air-conditioning repairers, tune-up techs, front-end mechanics, engine performance analysts or transmission technicians and rebuilders, to name a few.

Those new to automotive service usually start as trainee technicians, technician's helpers or lubrication workers. As their skills increase, or if they come into the workplace as a graduate of a post-secondary automotive training program, they can advance to the journey level and work toward becoming an established, qualified service technician. This may take two to five years of experience.

Another one to two years of experience allows the tech to become familiar with all types of repairs. That solid base of on-the-job training lets the tech move into complex specialties which require another year or two of training and experience. As the tech moves forward along the career track, he or she can work toward gaining all eight ASE certifications to achieve the Master Automobile Technician status.

Automotive Technicians with experience and administrative ability sometimes advance to become service managers or shop supervisors. Techs with good communications skills and who work well with customers may become automotive repair service estimators. Sometimes those with funds may even decide to open their own independent repair shops or buy into chain shops.

Work Schedules

Most automotive technicians work a standard forty hour week, although thirty percent work longer hours. Depending on the work waiting in-shop and the hours of the dealership service center or repair shop, techs may work evenings or weekends to satisfy customer and/or employer needs. Typical hours entail a nine-hour shift with an hour lunch break. A shift may start at six or seven in the morning to allow customers to drop off vehicles before work. Another shift may end as late as seven or eight in the evening, although often the work is finished before this time and the service or shop manager stays to take care of those picking up vehicles.

An automotive tech can expect similar hours working for the government. Sam Sepulveda, Fleet Manager for the United States Border Patrol, says, "Our garages work on a Monday to Friday, eight to five schedule. Our vehicles are used sometimes twenty-four hours seven days a week, depending on if there are any special operations where you have to have more people and more vehicles in a certain area. Basically that's the first thing on our minds -- officer safety. So if needed, we work overtime on Saturdays."

Supervisors and Service Managers, such as Cecil Hebert with Champion Toyota in Austin, Texas, sometimes work longer hours. "I'm usually here by seven in the morning and sometimes don't leave until six or seven at night. But that's my choice. I don't have to, but I'm a semi-workaholic. My schedule hours with the company are actually eight to six, but I'm here a lot of the time longer than that. I have two other managers under me and we rotate Saturdays. So I work one every three, just like they do. It's not too bad." It's different for the techs under him. "We have two shifts at this store because we're open 'til ten o'clock. Once the economy picks back up, we'll go back to being open until midnight. Our technicians come in at eight o'clock and leave at five and the second shift comes in at three and works 'til midnight. I have basically three technicians that come in at night and I have five light line techs or what we call lube rack work, entry level work. So, I've got eight guys that work the night shift with us. They rotate weekends, working every other Saturday. When they work a Saturday, I give them a day off the week they worked so they're not working more than five days a week."

With more experience and certifications, a tech can move up in ranking, possibly moving from being paid per hour to being paid on commission. Being paid on commission does not mean longer hours, but it can mean more money within the same time period. A tech becomes more knowledgeable and more productive as he gains experience and can work faster with fewer mistakes. Juan Avila, who works on diesels for Boggus Ford, says, "A gasoline tech may have to work over eight hours on three or four cars to make what I make on one truck in that same eight hours. With experience, I could probably work on two trucks, even three, in one day."

Employers

One thing that can put a job-seeker ahead of others is formal training in the field -- either completion of a high school program or a post-secondary vocational school or community college. More and more employers are looking for those highly trained automotive technicians coming out of a program with certification in-hand. They know that those AUTs already possess an array of workplace skills and have academic and technical skills as well. Employers prefer hiring AUTs who have completed classes in a program that stresses a real world approach to skill building with hands-on experience through mockups and modern vehicles. They not only have the necessary education skills, they have practiced them within the context of working on vehicles and preparing to enter the workforce. The National Automotive Technicians Education Foundation (NATEF) says, "With the advent of technology at an ever accelerating pace, there has been a rethinking regarding the most effective methodologies for teaching math, science and communication skills. Teaching those disciplines in the context of where and how people live and work is not only gaining in acceptance, but it is deemed critical to survival in a technology-imbued environment."

Part of what an employer of automotive technicians looks for in a potential employee is an inquisitive, sharp mind. Employers know that when someone chooses to enter the field he or she can expect a lifetime of learning. Technology evolves, changes, adapts and AUTs must keep up. Learning and training does not end with graduation. It continues through a lifetime and career.

Jack Taylor, Service Manager for Land Rover of Austin, tells the story of a young tech he hired right out of TSTC Waco. "He was a sponge -- always on the computer, absorbing everything. Within two years, this kid knew more about these cars than just about anyone. After four years, the factory engineers were calling him, asking what he thought about different problems. He's now a field engineer for Land Rover North America and consults with engineers out of England. He's still a sponge and the future is open for him."

Over the last few decades so much has changed in automotive technology that techs have to have more than just a thirst for knowledge about cars and how they run. They have to know mathematics, communication and problem-solving techniques. They need to be able to work solo and as part of a team. They also have to be honest, ethical and have a clean record. Jack Taylor, who currently has fourteen techs working for him at the Land Rover dealership, says, "When we hire someone, we run a background check and a drug screen. We're looking for character in a person. You have to have a clear driving record -- two tickets and I can't even hire you. Then once you're hired on, we run drivers' licenses every year. If you pick up two tickets, you're reprimanded and you get a written warning. Three tickets, you're terminated. We're looking for people who have the ambition, the drive, and the character to become part of the Land Rover family."

Teaching Lab Assistant Profile: Abel Castillo, Jr.

Abel Castillo's duties as a lab assistant include taking care of the shop equipment and helping with (and teaching) labs at TSTC Harlingen. He describes himself as a curious person who reads a lot. "Every time I read something, I learn something new. Even though I've been in the industry since 1992, I learn something every day." He also keeps up with the industry, going out to the shops and dealerships, asking questions and talking to supervisors and working techs. "We're a Ford program training center here at TSTC. Our techs work with a lot of different dealerships here in the Valley -- Toyota, BMW, Ford, Nissan. Some work while going to school. Some when they graduate go straight to work. Sometimes dealerships even come here to interview students. We, as instructors here, are always trying to work with industry. We get together with our advisory committee, which is made up of different managers and supervisors from dealers in the area, three times a year to talk about their needs -- what they want from us, what they want us to be focusing more on. That helps us out. And it helps them. We work tirelessly with industry. We couldn't make it without them and they couldn't make it without us."

Castillo loves what he does, but it wasn't always that way. "I started with my dad, cleaning parts with a brush and some diesel, and I hated it." He went to work in retail instead. Then he was hired by a dealership to work front end, taking care of customers and doing service writing. Even after attending dealer sponsored seminars, he still felt something was missing. He decided to go for his ASE certificates and college. Now he says, "I'm very responsible, very disciplined. I love what I do.

"Being a student and being in industry, I know what a student goes through when he's looking for a job. It's hard. It can be tough to find a job. I talk to the industry. I encourage them to give the students an opportunity to prove what they can do. Our students are fresh; they don't have any bad habits. They can be trained, sculpted. We teach the basics of automotive, and then they can train to be where they want them to be. It's very important for someone working in the industry, but who doesn't have the classes, to come and take the classes. It'll make him a technician, his job will grow, he can become a Master tech. In school, I was able to master my

ASE certifications. I wouldn't have done that without the school here."

Castillo tells students to "have a lot of patience. If you were able to make it through twelve years of school, then one or two or three years in an automotive technology program is nothing. It's just a matter of focusing, setting your goals, being very realistic about what's out there and doing your very best."

Analyze, Diagnose and Repair

An automotive technician has to be a good problem solver. Most customers who bring their vehicles into a repair shop or service area haven't a clue what's wrong. They only know something isn't right. The AUT has to analyze the situation, figure out the problem and then solve it. In other words, the AUT has to have the skills to analyze, diagnose and repair. Sounds simple, but while most people may be able to figure out they need a new oil filter and how to change one, it takes considerably more skill to analyze what's wrong with a clutch, diagnose the exact problem, pull it apart, fix the problem and then, showing quality workmanship, reassemble -- correctly, safely and in a timely manner.

The tech first gets a description of the problem from the owner of the vehicle or from the service adviser. Then the tech tests the problem components and systems and isolates the probable cause. Once the problem is diagnosed, the tech can set about remedying the situation.

A lot of the skill of being able to analyze, diagnose and repair comes through training. This is where schooling becomes invaluable. In classes in a post-secondary program, students are routinely given real-life problems to solve, not on paper or through theoretical situations but on actual vehicles and parts using tools and equipment that would be available on the job. Employers hiring graduating automotive technicians know they are taking on someone who has developed this skill set and will not have to be trained.

Above all, automotive tech *must be* able to troubleshoot.

Electronics and Computers

While electronics may conjure up images of the wiring in a house or hooking up cable TV, today's vehicles contain many electrical components, such as the electronic computer controlled distributor, electronic computer controlled shift and electronic fuel injectors.

Today, computers play a big role in the AUT's job. In modern repair shops, computers are commonplace. Service technicians use computerized diagnostic testing devices then compare the readout with benchmarked standards given by the manufacturer. Most shops receive automatic updates to manuals and access manufacturers' service information and technical bulletins through the Internet or from software.

Computers are playing a bigger and bigger role in the high tech cars of today, operating everything from the radio to the engine. Computers and electronic components control braking, transmission, steering systems, integrated global positioning systems, even on-board Internet service. Not only do today's techs have to know electronics and computers in order to use the diagnostic equipment in their shops, they have to know how to work on the electronics and computers in the vehicles themselves.

The automotive tech of today has to be familiar with computers and electronics and be ready to adapt to new advances.

Mechanical

Even though computers play a major role in today's cars and their repair, an AUT still has to have a knowledge of and skill with machines and tools, including their designs, uses, repair and maintenance.

As you might surmise, those talented people who work on automobiles accumulate and work with an array of tools that the average person wouldn't have a clue how to use. AUTs who come from a post-secondary program begin to collect tools while in school. For classes and skill units, they purchase bench units, such as carburetors, starters, alternators, air conditioning compressors, power steering pumps, manual and power steering gear boxes, and tandem master cylinders. They buy and become familiar with things like brake fluid, welding rods and oils.

In class they use laboratory equipment and instruments including digital volt ohm meters, digital storage oscilloscopes, graphing digital multimeters, personal computers, five-gas exhaust analyzers and engine analyzers, brake lathes, drum and outside disc micrometers, computerized four-wheel alignment systems, hydraulic lifts and automotive computer diagnostic scanning tools. Many post-secondary programs partner with automobile manufacturers to make this equipment available to students. Texas State Technical College Waco has up-to-date equipment and laboratories worth approximately $3 million.

Automotive technicians must possess mechanical aptitude and a knowledge of how automobiles work.

AUT Service Manager Profile: Jack Taylor

Jack Taylor has always loved cars, but he didn't start his working career in the automotive industry. He began in direct sales where he has extensive training. Eventually, though, he came around to the car business, starting as a Service Advisor. Now the Service Manager for Land Rover of Austin, he has been in the auto industry for thirty-one years. "I grew up building race cars. We held NHRA national records. As far as formal training, mine has been in management in the sales end. The technician part of it I've learned along the way by going to technical schools through Land Rover and reviewing and working with technicians every day on fixing cars."

Taylor says, "We have fourteen techs working right now. I set up my shop so the techs run the ticket. In other words, they do everything to the car from the time they get their work order, from state inspections to engine overhauls. It doesn't matter -- wind noises, water leaks, electrical problems -- they run the whole car. I make sure they're cross-trained in the whole vehicle so the techs have the knowledge, confidence and hands-on experience to make decisions."

When looking to hire a tech, Taylor turns to graduates of a post-secondary program, primarily TSTC Waco. "The future of our business is people who have made that commitment and put in the time and money, and have already given part of their life to that deal."

According to Taylor, graduates have a solid base of the fundamentals of how cars work. "I've seen the dedication of the instructors at TSTC Waco to their students. They care about them. The students get a solid knowledge base at TSTC, then we put them into Land Rover's Web-based training program. There are about twenty different tests they take as part of their continuing education. Also, they're paired with a senior tech to watch and learn. We leave the trainee there for sixty to ninety days, and then move him to another senior tech. One tech may be more efficient in heavy line. Another may be more efficient in electrical. Over the course of about a year, the trainee gets an overall view, practices efficiency and learns the best skills of each senior tech. Then he's ready to work on his own."

Jack Taylor does see one national problem with techs: "There are not enough."

Physical

Despite the increasing use of computers in diagnosing problems and in the vehicles themselves, the everyday job of an AUT is not one where she or he sits behind a computer for long stretches of time. For the most part, the job of an AUT is physical.

Sometimes he must work in awkward positions and lift heavy parts and tools. She has to have the ability to climb, balance, stoop and kneel. There might be minor cuts and bruises or burns, but serious accidents can be avoided through safe work practices. An AUT must be aware of hazardous materials control -- this is something that is stressed both in school and on the job.

Good hand-to-eye coordination is needed to work with hand tools, computerized shop equipment and electronic components. Automotive technicians should have the necessary color discrimination to differentiate wire and resistance color codes. Near visual acuity and depth perception is needed when working with small parts. Even hearing is important since AUTs should be capable of discovering, analyzing and correcting irregular vehicle noises.

While an AUT does not have to be a body builder or have perfect vision without correction, an automotive technician should be in good physical condition and ready to tackle the job.

Mental

Critical thinking is important for an automotive technician. He or she needs to be able to use logic and reasoning to identify the strengths and weaknesses of alternative solutions, conclusions or approaches to problems. The AUT needs to be ready to identify complex problems and review related information to develop and evaluate options and implement solutions. To that end, she has to understand written sentences and paragraphs in work-related documents and manuals. Often, this means the AUT must work independently, developing his own way of doing things, without supervision, to complete tasks. When there are obstacles, he or she must analyze, use logic and work around them. What this means is that an AUT must know what he's doing, learn what he doesn't know and use that knowledge to improvise when necessary.

An AUT must also be able to communicate with others. Working on automobiles is rarely a solitary job. The automotive technician talks to other technicians. Sometimes he interacts with customers. Those with good interpersonal skills are often moved into the position of service manager or repair service estimator. As an automotive technician moves up in her certification toward the Master level, she may be in the position to teach others who are coming up behind her.

An AUT must exercise his brain muscles every day on the job.

AUT Working Tech Profile: Chris Palacios

Chris Palacios has a lot of training and experience in this field. He spent ten years in the Navy working on jet engines, then he graduated from Universal Technical Institute, worked for a Toyota dealership where he won a scholarship to the T-TEN program at San Jacinto College, and soon afterward joined Westside Lexus in Houston, Texas.

"The automotive technology field is not your father's, grandfather's, even great-grandfather's, car any more where you can be a shade tree mechanic, sit under the shade tree and exchange spark plugs, change the oil and then you're done. You have to know how to read a computer, the basics of electricity, how to read a wiring diagram. It's pretty intense. I enjoy it because maybe there's something out there that somebody can't fix and I was able to fix it. Doing it is where I get my greatest joy. I can see something I did. I made that car run."

Palacios admits going to school is not always easy. "I've seen people quit. You have not only your automotive program, but your academics and that's what's real hard on a person. There have been nights where I stayed up to two or three o'clock in the morning and I've got to go a full day the next day. But, you know, this is what I want." When Palacios started at Toyota and was thinking of going to the T-TEN program at San Jacinto College, his mentor encouraged him. "He said, 'It's the best thing.' If you wait, it's going to take you seven to ten years to get all those credentials. If you sacrifice just two small years of your life, it's the best thing you can ever do. It's just two years. Two years is nothing. Two years is a sneeze in a lifetime."

Not through with learning, Palacios currently has five ASE certifications. "I plan to work for the other three to get my Masters." If he could talk to incoming techs, he would tell them to keep learning. "Some things are kind of basic, but I've been doing this for quite a while. I see some of the new guys coming in, the apprentices, and they kind of have a tough time because they don't understand how something works. It's like electricity. How does electricity work? How does it ground if you have rubber tires? How does the airplane ground if it's in the air? A lot of people don't understand that. And a lot of people don't really think about it. But to us, if we have static electricity in the car which keeps shocking the customer, or the radio keeps flicking in and out, we have to know where that ground's at and what's wrong with it."

He recommends getting an AAS degree and also dealership programs. "It's good to specialize because then you can stay in that small family and that small family can help you grow."

Honesty and Ethics

Graduates of a two-year automotive technology program can earn an average annual starting salary of around $40,000. With on-the-job experience, earnings can increase substantially, depending on specialization, location and company size. Metropolitan areas, due to their high population, usually offer more opportunities and higher starting salaries. Whether a tech works on all areas of a vehicle or specializes often depends on whether he works for a small, independent shop or a huge dealership.

No matter whether she works for a small shop or a multi-million dollar dealership, the AUT is a professional. Like all professionals, automotive technicians are honest and ethical in their dealings with customers, fellow techs and management. Their honesty contributes to whether and how far they advance in their careers. Being honest and ethical is a source of pride for the auto tech.

As a student leaves school and enters the workforce, he finds that high standards of professionalism are set within the workplace. With the high expectation of professionalism comes great potential for advancement.

An automotive technician is honest with his partners, his boss and his customers. Most of all, an automotive tech is honest with himself.

Other Skills

In addition to the skills and knowledge mentioned previously, automotive technicians should also have mathematical skills. An AUT not only has to read and study manuals and work on a computer, he has to estimate automotive repair costs and time as well as order replacement parts. If the service repair estimator has already estimated the cost of the repair work, including the AUT's hours, then the tech must take that into consideration when ordering parts and accumulating his work time.

An AUT must be able to manage stress. Problems arise, vehicles needing work stack up, some jobs need more attention and focus than others, customers are angry, other workers or managers have bad days, personal problems creep into the workplace, parts don't show up as expected, aches plague knees and a million things go wrong. With as many problems as the AUT has to solve during the course of a workday, he needs to be able to manage stress so he can stay calm, focused and productive, as well as happy in his job and working well with others.

Maintaining an orderly work area is important for both the tech and those working around him. Equipment, machines, wiring and programs should be installed to specification. Putting tools away after use means it's easier to find those tools the next time they're needed -- and makes the clean up faster at the end of the day. Tools put away are also less likely to be lost or disappear. Tools are expensive to replace. Cleaning up spills not only keeps your area neat, it can help prevent accidents. Keeping the work area straightened during the day makes the job easier, faster, more efficient, and just as important, shows your professionalism.

Conclusion

According to O*Net, the following skills ranked in the top twenty percent of requirements for Master Automotive Technicians:

1. Mechanical
2. Computers and Electronics
3. Customer and Personal Service
4. Education and Training
5. Troubleshooting
6. Repairing
7. Equipment Selection
8. Active Learning
9. Reading Comprehension
10. Critical Thinking
11. Complex Problem Solving
12. Installation
13. Active Listening
14. Repairing and Maintaining Mechanical Equipment

The average person has no clue how the automobile works. They just expect it to miraculously run. It is the automotive technician who makes the magic happen. It is the AUT's skill, knowledge, finesse and hard work that keep the cars and trucks of the world running smoothly.

The automotive technician with skills will advance in his career and will find satisfaction in his work.

AUT Employer Profile: Cecil Hebert

Cecil Hebert has been in the automotive industry since 1981, starting at his father's shop then moving into Toyota dealerships. For the past five years, he's been with Champion Toyota in Austin, Texas, where he is the Service Manager. He's on the Gulf States Region of Toyota Dealerships Parts and Service dealer advisory council for the National Dealer council and is also on TSTC Waco's T-TEN Technology Automotive Program committee. He describes himself as an "extrovert," someone who likes to "interact with people." That's definitely a good thing since he has ninety-three employees working under him, fifty-one of whom are techs.

When he interviews possible new techs, he, of course, looks at the training they've had. Beyond the basics like math and diagnostics, he also considers attitude, character and how the applicant carries himself. "I look for a team player. I like to hear the 'we' attitude. I also quiz them very hard about what brought them to this industry, which has become very technical, very computer oriented. I'd rather have somebody in here with a great attitude than with a full blown load of experience." Hebert also talks to the tech's teachers. "The better impression they make on the instructor, the better impression it's going to make on the people hiring them."

New techs, primarily students or graduates of a T-TEN program, coming to Champion Toyota are paired up with either a Master level or an MDT level technician. They're put into a light line position doing repeat work like oil change and tires and start out working at an hourly rate, forty hours a week. Once they gain experience, Hebert weans them off the hourly wage. "We start having them flag hours, but we're still paying them hourly. Once we see that they're producing enough hours to make more money or at least make a decent living, then we put them on commission hours. It's more like a mentoring program, but they're actually working with that technician." Depending on the pace of the tech, this weaning process can take from three to nine months. "I had one that was put on the line in probably a month."

Hebert says, "Entry-level commission rates usually, at least at this store, start at $13.50 to $14.50 an hour. That's entry level whenever they start flagging work. Then you can go up to twenty-four, twenty-five, twenty-six dollars an hour and you've got guys who can do that water pump the book says takes two and a half hours in an hour. So they're actually getting two and a half hour's pay for an hour's work. That's where you start making the money. Time and experience can actually get you there. I've got technicians who can make a hundred thousand a year and I've got some who can only make thirty or forty."

He suggests techs do some research before starting their job applications. "Go to your local dealership or independent shop, if you can, and quiz them on everything. Find out about the business. It's all specialized stuff now. You're not going to fix these cars today with a wrench or pair of pliers anymore."

Hebert takes time to get to know the people who work for him. "We spend more time together than we do with our families." He looks for techs who are compassionate and who love people the way he does. "If you want to be in a people job, this is the place to be."

Chapter 2: Automotive Technician Education & Certification

Not all that long ago, automotive technology was taught in high schools as an optional vocational class. Students spent class time working on projects, doing repairs or break-downs, and getting an elective grade. The hands-on approach was the primary method of teaching. Today, automotive technology goes beyond the high school level and is taught in secondary programs, in community colleges and four-year universities. It is taught not just as a way for teens to work on their cars, but as a career opportunity. As automotive technology advances, so do the methodologies for teaching it. Chris Tran, first-year instructor, says, "I love teaching in the T-TEN program at San Jac. In the classroom, I present the lecture, the PowerPoint, then once we learn, we're off to the lab. The students pair up and work together. If they have a question, they'll raise their hand and call me. I'll come and help or answer. They have lab sheets and they have to follow the directions. Some things can be done quickly. Some, like the engine class, can take the whole semester to tear it all the way down and put it back together. It helps them to work in the dealership. They can see, they can relate, and they are more likely to want to try it."

AUTs now have to have both hand and head skills. Today's automotive technology programs reflect that by integrating math, science and communication skills into the teaching. The automobiles of today are complex and technologically driven. Today's instructors realize that and are preparing student AUTs for this advanced world.

Post-secondary automotive technology programs teach the student more than the parts and repair of an automobile's components. They teach the student to analyze and think for himself. For example, to earn an Associate of Applied Science degree in Automotive Technology, a TSTC student must pass her core tech classes, as well as courses in composition, humanities, social and behavioral sciences, math and others. Austin Community College (ACC) AUT students take classes in speech, English, math and, for an enhanced skills certificate, small business management. St. Phillip's asks their AUT students to complete classes in math and social and behavioral sciences or communication. Some programs are now offering classes on customer service, stressing management and other employability skills. As the education of today's automotive technicians has increased in depth and breadth, so has the respect and occupational outlook.

AUT Supervisor Profile: Robert Parnell

After three decades in the automotive business, Robert Parnell, Parts and Service Director at Westside Lexus in Houston, Texas, has a glassed-in office and is highly respected. But he started out at a time when there weren't many college level courses in auto mechanics. "I got out of high school and was very interested in cars, so I went to work for a local parts house. Actually techs made more money and if, back then, an opportunity like this had existed, I would have jumped on it. But there wasn't anything like this around thirty-five years ago, and so I just never did make it into becoming a technician. I went from parts to going into service administration. I've been doing this for thirty-five years and I enjoy it today more than I did thirty-five years ago. It's been a great experience."

Parnell recommends that anyone interested in becoming an automotive technician take classes. "In the last ten years, we've not hired a trainee that didn't have a vocational course. There are a couple of kids we've hired out of high school VOTEC programs but as a condition of employment, we require them to go to that secondary education. In the long run, they're just not going to be super successful without it. A bachelor's degree would give them an edge if they want to be in management."

At Westside Lexus, Parnell supervises fifty technicians who work in lateral support groups. Each team has four techs ranging in experience from the group leader, an ASE Master tech, to the newest tech just out of the T-TEN program. Not only do these groups provide support for new techs and mentors for them to turn to, Westside Lexus offers incentives for technicians to achieve their ASE certificates. Parnell says, "We offer task bonuses for the completion of each one of those ASE certificates -- and then an additional task for the Master status. The bonuses will affect your pay but if you pass the test we offer a reimbursement for the cost of the test and then we give you a $50 bonus. We talk about it a lot in our meetings and we promote the ASE certifications. We think they're great. It just says a lot about you as a technician. It says, I am a professional committed to my industry."

Based on his personal experience and his decades of work in the industry, he recommends young people interested in automotive technology start early -- in high school if possible. "Definitely go to the secondary education program. It's a great field. It's very rewarding, very challenging, and there are lots of opportunities for those people willing to work hard."

Educational Requirements

While some students get jobs right out of high school, learning as apprentices by assisting and working with experienced mechanics, others decide to go beyond high school for formal education. Because automotive technology is rapidly increasing in sophistication, most training authorities recommend that persons seeking automotive technician jobs complete a formal program after graduating from high school. Some get an associate degree through a two-year program at a community or technical college. Others go for a four-year bachelor's degree.

Associate of Applied Science, Automotive Technology

Many schools offer a one-year Certificate of Completion and a Specialized Certificate of Completion or Enhanced Skills Certificate -- this program provides intensive career preparation through classroom instruction and hands-on practice. This often leads to a two-year program:

- A two-year degree based on tech classes and academic courses, either classes only or classes combined with paid work experience.

- A partnership and internship with an automobile manufacturer, such as Toyota or Chrysler -- students in this degree plan typically spend three to six weeks per semester working full time in service departments of sponsoring dealers.

Bachelor of Science, Automotive Technology

Most students with a BS in Automotive Technology graduate to hold positions in automotive related industries, including field service operations, fleet management and technical support activities.

The most common post-secondary path to automotive technology certification is obtaining an Associate of Applied Science (AAS) degree. After completing courses in a post-secondary program, graduates may apply for various professional certifications offered by organizations such as the National Institute for Automotive Service Excellence (ASE) and the Automatic Transmission Rebuilders Association (ATRA).

The ASE Automobile/Light Truck Test Series includes eight certification exams:

1. Engine Repair
2. Automatic Transmission/Transaxle
3. Manual Drive Train and Axles
4. Suspension and Steering
5. Brakes
6. Electrical/Electronic Systems
7. Heating and Air Conditioning
8. Engine Performance

To become ASE certified, technicians must pass one or more of the automobile exams and present proof of at least two years of relevant work experience. Those who pass all eight exams are recognized as ASE-certified Master Automobile Technicians. Technicians may substitute two years of relevant formal training for up to one year of the work experience requirement.

Currently, there are post-secondary programs offering degrees and certification in Automotive Technology in every state in the U.S. See http://www.natef.org/certified00.cfm for a complete list of NATEF/ASE Certified Programs.

AUT Instructor Profile: Homer Swihart

"Some of my earliest, fondest memories are working on Volkswagen Bugs with my dad in my driveway when I was a young child. Many a night we fell asleep underneath the car in the winter with the warmth of the big spotlights." Until he was around sixteen years old, Homer Swihart helped his dad keep the family cars running, but says he didn't do it just because it was his dad. "I was intrigued with automobiles and how they worked. I loved it."

Married at nineteen, Swihart knew he had to support his family. He and his wife collected aluminum cans for six months to pay for his first semester at San Jacinto College, but when he told his instructor, David Norman, that he couldn't afford to come back the next semester, Norman offered to show him how to apply for partial payment plans, which allowed Swihart to continue. He didn't find out until many years later that Norman had so much faith in Swihart that he had paid the initial deposit on the partial payment out of his own pocket.

Although it took Swihart sixteen years to finish his two-year associate degree, his first-year instructor's belief in him was well justified. He's now San Jac's Toyota T-TEN Coordinator and Lead Instructor in the Automotive Technology Department. Homer Swihart is one of the few T-TEN instructors in the world who has also achieved MDT, Master Diagnostic Technician, certification.

He didn't set out to achieve this elite position. "The MDT is only for Toyota techs and you have to be a Master L1 certified technician, have completed all of their electronic or online factory training and completed all of their factory training that you go to school for." Plus, you have to be employed by Toyota or by a Toyota dealer. Swihart had already decided to do the near impossible -- teach full time, run the Toyota program at San Jac and work in a dealership so that he would know what his students went through when they apprenticed. Swihart says, "There was a lot of sacrifice that came with that -- working eight hours a day, then coming to San Jac and working eight hours at night, for almost a year. Lot of hard work and a lot of sleepless nights."

Then he was told he qualified to take the MDT test. "This test took almost three weeks to do, off and on, about two or three hours a day. If you can't do the work, you can't pass because the majority of the test is about looking up information on the Toyota information center and knowing how to read a diagram. There was a lot of research involved. It was a tough test. You have to renew it every two years."

His life and work has shaped him into an instructor who cares about his students. "The only thing I can think of that's better than working on cars is teaching young people who love it too how to do what I did for twenty-something years." Since taking over San Jac's Toyota program six years ago, Swihart and his students created the motto Build, Steer and Cheer. "We build, steer and cheer these students as they come in. I've spent a lot of weekends here working on academics with them, spent a lot of break time sitting in here, encouraging them and telling them that this too will pass, let's keep going, just put one foot in front of the other, go home tonight and get some sleep, we'll attack it tomorrow, don't let it get you down." But Swihart doesn't worry too much about the hours he puts in. "The truth is, it's not work for me to come in here and talk to these kids. It's what I love to do."

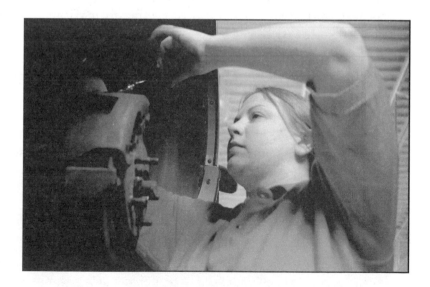

The Two-Year Associate of Applied Science Degree

The Associate of Applied Science degree in Automotive Technology prepares the student to perform bumper-to-bumper diagnostics as well as repair, testing and preventive maintenance on automobiles and light trucks. This on-the-job training along with classroom instruction prepares students for careers as automotive technicians. In most programs, sixty to seventy percent of a student's time is spent working with equipment and vehicles. If the student follows the work cooperative/internship route, that time includes working at a repair facility or dealer's shop. In addition to hands-on training, students take classes designed to help them in the workforce and in comprehensive and critical theory. A typical AAS degree in automotive technology requires sixty-six credit hours, completed over a twenty-month (five semester) period. After earning an Associate of Applied Science degree, graduates work in service centers and dealerships and have the education necessary for promotion or additional responsibilities.

AUT Instructor Profile: Chris Tran

Chris Tran, first-year instructor for the T-TEN program at San Jacinto College in Pasadena, Texas started teaching in 2008, but he's been in the automotive field for years. "I went through San Jac in 1990-something, then worked out in the field for thirteen years. I worked in two dealerships, both Toyota. I was one of the main techs. When I first started out I was the lowest tech, because I didn't know much. But as time went by, I learned more and more, became trained and got better."

He advises his students, "They'll start you at the bottom, but in a few months your supervisors or mentors may see that you're good and they'll move you up pretty quickly. But if you're still not getting it or are weak at something, then you need more training."

Needing additional training isn't necessarily a negative, Tran believes. "If a student is trying to learn and he's trying really hard and he finally gets it, that's the one we want to train. The one that doesn't care, that's the one you know won't last. If you don't care here, you're not going to care out there in the real world. And you're not going to make it. You've got to make it here and understand what we're doing here, then take it with you out there on the job."

Tran is a strong advocate for students achieving their associate degree. "People think it's just nuts and bolts, but it's math, formulas, chemistry, geometry, physics; it's all combined. The Toyota T-TEN program has its courses, then there are the academics -- history, government, English, math. Students have to take those, too, for the associate degree. If you just want to take the T-TEN program, then you'll get a certificate. Now, with a certificate, your level's going to be down here. With a degree, you'll be up here and you'll advance faster."

Even instructors continue their education and advancement. Already a Master technician, Tran is going for his L1. He also teaches dual credit at one of the local high schools. "I teach the juniors. What they learn here will count as college credit plus high school credit. My students come here three days a week, seven to nine in the morning before their own school starts. I get here at six in the morning to get ready. The eleventh graders are still not sure what they want to do. This is like a test drive. If they like it, they continue. If not, they go for something else."

Tran loves teaching. "I like everything about my job. I like the way it's laid out and the way, as a teacher, I stand up and try to show them, encourage them, so later on they can be a success. This is what I want to do -- try to help whoever wants to be a success."

The Four-Year Bachelor's Degree

For those aspiring to enter the industry as technical representatives, service managers, specialized diagnosticians, or in similar mid-management positions with companies such as Ford, GM, General Electric and Toyota, a four-year degree is the quickest way. Students can minor in areas that allow exploration of interests that complement the automotive major and choose electives that will enhance their communication and organizational abilities. In a typical four-year degree plan, a total of 130 credit hours is required, with a minimum of sixty-three of those within the automotive technology program. The credit hours to satisfy the major in automotive technology might be broken down into automotive service courses, automotive technology courses, sales and service courses, support courses and electives. The remaining credit hours would come from the general requirements of the school for a Bachelor of Science degree.

The choice between a two-year and a four-year program comes down to career plans and the amount of time and money the tech decides to spend.

Whether considering a two-year or a four-year post-secondary program, it is important to verify that the program is certified. The National Automotive Technicians Education Foundation (NATEF), founded in 1983, evaluates and recommends qualifying programs for accreditation by ASE. Although NATEF does not endorse specific curricular materials, it does set standards for the content of instruction, which includes tasks, tools and equipment, hours and instructor qualifications. By going online at http://www.natef.org/certified.cfm, anyone considering a two- or four-year program can check that school's certification.

AUT Student/Working Tech Profile: Juan P. Avila

"I'm the type of kid who liked to take things apart and put them back together to see how they work," says Juan Avila. "I like working with kids; I like working with people. And I think I'd like to be an instructor, especially in automotive."

He's almost finished with his associate degree at TSTC Harlingen and is working on getting his ASE certifications. He knows that working in the automotive technology field can be intimidating. "It's okay to be scared, especially if you've never done it before. But if you like it, if you're into it, take it apart and just write down where everything goes. It's nice. I enjoy it."

While going to school, Avila works for a dealership. "Right now, I work on diesels. We get paid on commission. Diesels are heavy work. Dirty. I wasn't used to that. At my previous dealership I worked on Lincolns where you have to be clean, your shirt tucked in. On diesels, you can't stay clean. Now that I'm working on diesels, I wouldn't go back to work on gasoline cars. The money is in diesels. A whole lot more money. It's dirty, it's heavy work, but the money's right there for a technician."

When Avila thinks about the future of automotive technology, he says, "I believe there will always be a need for technicians because there are people who don't know how to work on their vehicles because they're so complicated. The hybrids are big now. On today's vehicles, about twenty-five percent is mechanical and the other seventy-five percent is electrical. There are so many modules now in vehicles."

On a personal level, Avila says, "Being positive will help you a lot. I had good mentors and that makes me want to be a good mentor if I ever get a helper to work under me or it comes to the day when I teach. And I know I'm going to teach. My dad taught me how to work. If I want something, I have to work for it. That's what I'm doing for my kids now." He's putting that philosophy into practice with plans beyond his associate degree. "I don't want to stop there. I want to get my four-year degree -- just to make it a little better, get into Psychology so I can learn to work with the kids. I think that will help me. Ever since I was a little kid, I knew I wanted to work with people, be a counselor. And I think with teaching I could do that." And he'd still be able to stay in the automotive field.

Tuition & Fees

An automotive technology student can expect to pay around $65 per course hour for in-state tuition in Texas. Out-of-state tuition, however, can triple that figure. An Associate of Applied Science degree in Automotive Technology, a total of sixty-six credit hours at most schools, can be achieved in around five semesters. With summer school, the degree can be earned in about twenty months, less than two years. As in any technology program, there is also the cost of books and equipment, such as bench units and hand tools. Those hand tools are purchased over the course of the two years and go with the tech into his or her future job.

There is help, though. A community college, like all colleges, may be able to help with financial assistance. This is something a potential student should check out with his or her high school counselor or the college admittance office. If, as a high school student, the tech has been working for a shop or dealership, that employer may be willing to help with assistance in tuition, with the understanding that the graduating tech will return and even perhaps continue to work as she goes to classes.

A great many colleges offering degrees in Automotive Technology partner with vehicle manufacturers and dealerships to offer specific training, paid cooperative education opportunities, scholarships and tools, and assistance in finding a position within a dealership after graduation. To find out if the school under consideration has a partnership program, check the school's web site to see if they offer such programs as:

- Toyota-Technical Education Network (T-TEN)

- Chrysler College Automotive Program (CAP)

- BMW Service Technician Education Program (STEP)

- Honda Professional Automotive Career Training (PACT)

- Mercedes-Benz Enthusiasm, Loyalty, Integrity, Talent, Excellence (ELITE)

- GM Service Technical College (STC)

Another place to find out about these programs is the Automotive Youth Educational Systems (AYES) Web site at: https://www.ayes.org/.

Increasingly, employers are willing to pay or help in the cost of sending their experienced automotive service technicians to manufacturer training centers for special training in the repair of components or of new models. Even beginning technicians may be offered the opportunity by dealerships to attend training programs to update their skills. Sometimes working techs can gain training on the job, when factory representatives visit the shop.

There's also good news for students just starting out in a post-secondary program. Graduating with an Associate of Applied Science degree in Automotive Technology demonstrates to a potential employer three things:

1. The tech has had active, hands-on experience working on vehicles.

2. The tech has learned auxiliary skills like reading manuals, communicating clearly and mathematics.

3. The tech knows this is the career s/he wants.

Students attending a community college can look into financial aid usually associated with four-year universities, like government assistance such as Pell grants. The Federal Pell Grant Program provides need-based grants at any one of approximately 5,400 participating post-secondary institutions. Undergraduate and vocational students enrolled or accepted for enrollment in participating schools may apply.

Don't overlook scholarship programs that help to defray cost. In addition to checking out the college you plan to attend, look to local businesses or organizations that give out scholarships. This is not to say you should overlook national or regional scholarships, but your chances are usually better with a local group. So start local and then search outside your hometown. Students are rarely limited to one source of financial aid.

If, as a high school student, you know automotive technology is the job you want to work in, check to see if your local community college offers dual credit courses in this field. Often, if you live in the community college's district, you can take these courses for no or little cost as a junior or senior and receive full college credit. If your high school offers Automotive Youth Educational Systems (AYES), become part of this group. More than likely, your AYES program works closely with a nearby college offering a degree in automotive technology, perhaps even dual credit courses. By doing this, you save

money and get a head start on your college hours.
Even if your high school has no partnership with
a community college, AYES has resources you can
turn to.

Students should always check with the school they
plan to attend to see if they offer scholarships,
reduced tuition packages or financial help. Some
schools offer reduced tuition packages for
non-resident students. Some have scholarships
exclusive to their college. Search the college's Web site
for information, then talk to a campus coordinator
for details.

Financial Aid

<u>Homer Swihart</u>

As head of San Jacinto College's T-TEN program, Homer Swihart gives out six scholarships each year. Those scholarships can include enough to cover a student's entire education and tools. With each of those scholarships, Swihart works hard at choosing hard-working and deserving recipients. "We can be a part of changing a kid's life. And in doing so, we change his whole family." Swihart adds, "We don't come in here and teach. We come in here with the attitude of changing lives. We don't go sit down at night and go, that kid's not going to make it. We say, if we don't help this kid, he's not going to make it. What can we do?"

<u>Robert Parnell</u>

As Parts and Service Director of Westside Lexus in Houston, Robert Parnell does more than just supervise student techs. He works to get them through their training. "Students work three or four hours a day, five days a week. In some cases, only four if they need to study because with the program they sometimes take academic classes along with the technical courses. But we're really flexible, we'll work with them any way we can. If they're interested in going to the T-TEN program, then we're willing to support them to get there however they want to do it. If they only want to work two hours a day, that's fine with us. Some of them work on Saturdays, that's kind of optional. We just do that to support the program. They're not really profitable to us at that point from a revenue point of view, but our gamble is that at some point down the road, they're going to make somebody a great technician -- hopefully us, and in many cases, that's the way it turns out to be."

<u>Chris Palacios</u>

Now a working technician at Westside Lexus of Houston, Palacios started in the Navy working on jet engines, then worked at a Toyota dealership. "I was in the Navy for ten years and when I got out I didn't really have a plan. I wasn't really prepared because I was medically discharged. So I was kind of thrown out into the world. When I was at Toyota,

> my manager offered me the opportunity to go to T-TEN. And
> I gladly accepted. I had to fill out the documents. I had to get
> references. And I ended up winning a scholarship. I went to
> T-TEN, graduated, and then maybe two months later, I came
> to this dealership. I have the best of both worlds. I specialize
> in Toyotas and Lexus."

ASE Certification

ASE (National Institute for Automotive Service
Excellence) is the standard for automotive
technology certification. This independent, non-profit
organization was established in 1972 with the mission
"to improve the quality of vehicle repair and service
through the testing and certification of repair and
service professionals."

The ASE Automobile and Light Truck Test Series
includes eight certification exams:

- Engine Repair (A1)

- Automatic Transmission/Transaxle (A2)
  Manual

- Drive Train and Axles (A3)

- Suspension and Steering (A4)

- Brakes (A5)

- Electrical/Electronic Systems (A6)

- Heating and Air Conditioning (A7)

- Engine Performance (A8)

To become ASE certified, technicians must pass one or more of the automobile exams and present proof of at least two years of relevant work experience. Those who pass all eight exams are recognized as ASE-certified Master Automobile Technicians. Each of the eight exams contain from forty to fifty questions. The written tests are offered two times a year, in May and November. You can also take computer-based tests at testing centers in January/February and July/August. To remain certified, those with ASE credentials must be retested every five years.

After achieving Master status, some techs go on to complete the Advanced Engine Performance Specialist Test (L1).

Some schools require students pass one or more ASE exams prior to graduation. Some do not require their students be certified in any of the eight categories. Some schools have their own in-house certifications in place of or in coordination with the ASE exams. But it is the ASE certifications that are recognized in the industry and it is the blue and white ASE insignia that is recognized by the public. Schools that encourage or require students to take ASE exams will usually recommend they take each test as close as possible to when that unit is being taught.

Questions on all ASE certification exams are written by service industry experts. All questions are job-related and designed to test the skills, not theoretical knowledge. In order to pass each test, a tech needs three types of knowledge and skills:

1. Basic technical knowledge
2. Service or repair knowledge and skill
3. Testing and diagnostic knowledge and skill.

ASE maintains a Web site with information about certification, including how to prepare for the tests, study guides and test tips (see http://www.ase.com/ Content/NavigationMenu/Service_Professionals1/ Prepare_to_Test/Prepare_to_Test.htm.)

As a student or beginning tech, gaining certifications shows potential employers that you are knowledgeable and are committed to a career in automotive technology. It also shows customers that they are entrusting their vehicle into capable hands. And most of all, it shows the tech that s/he has the knowledge and skill of a professional.

Students working in dealerships or shops in an apprentice program can often get reimbursed for the cost of the exam, as well as receive a boost in pay. Once a student graduates and goes to work full time in the field, the benefits increase. On its Web site, ASE lists the top ten reasons to become ASE certified:

1. Certification grants you professional credentials;
2. Certification demonstrates your commitment to the automotive service and repair profession;
3. Certification enhances the profession's image;
4. Certification reflects achievement;
5. Certification builds self-esteem;
6. Certification can improve career opportunities and advancement;
7. Certification may provide for greater earnings potential;
8. Certification improves skills and knowledge;
9. Certification prepares you for greater on-the-job responsibilities; and
10. Certification offers greater recognition from peers.

ASE Master Certification

Probably the most sought after and widely recognized ASE certification is the Master level. Achieving this certification can take anywhere from two to five years. To become a Master Automotive Technician, all eight ASE certifications must be passed and the tech must have met the hands-on working experience requirement. Being a Master Tech can mean an increase in pay as well as responsibility and prestige. Just about all shops and dealerships encourage their techs to earn their Master certification. It is not only good for the tech but also beneficial to the shop.

Cecil Hebert, Service Manager for Champion Toyota, Austin, Texas, prefers techs to have at least some of the eight ASE certifications before coming to work for him, but recognizes that it takes more than book learning to achieve the Master level. "Sometimes the book knowledge doesn't get the tech where he needs to be for the ASE test because a lot of the test requires hands-on knowledge. You learn by actually doing it." Hebert says his techs have to be at least working toward their certifications. In addition to ASE certifications, Toyota has its own in-house certifications. "We do evaluations at the end of every year and an increase in manufacturer's certification level or ASEs can be based toward a merit increase. An ASE Master level tech who's also a Toyota Master is going to make more. Getting certifications is the career path you want to follow to make more money."

The Master certification is not a separate test, but the culmination of the 8 ASE certifications:

- Engine Repair (A1)

- Automatic Transmission/Transaxle (A2)

- Manual Drive Train and Axles (A3)

- Suspension and Steering (A4)

- Brakes (A5)

- Electrical/Electronic Systems (A6)

- Heating and Air Conditioning (A7)

- Engine Performance (A8)

After passing all eight exams and accumulating the necessary work experience, a Master Tech proudly wears his Master patch or displays his certificates. He or she has reached a high level of skill, knowledge and perseverance.

AUT Student Profile: Mike Stapleton

"I've been interested in working on vehicles since junior high. Maybe even before that. My dad has a bunch of sports cars and cars have always fascinated me," says Mike Stapleton, first year student in the T-TEN program at San Jacinto College and working tech at Westside Lexus in Houston, Texas. "My first ASE test is in January and I'm expecting to pass. That test, I believe, is an engines test. I'm taking engines in T-TEN, so it's only smart to take the test while I'm taking the course." Stapleton is dedicated to this career, taking both automotive and academic classes toward an associate degree, working at a dealership and studying for class work and ASE exams. "San Jac requires four of them before you graduate and I'm required to take one every semester -- at least one."

He likes the challenges in the automotive technology field. "To be good at it, you have to know a lot of things. You have to grow with the technology. That's something else I like about it. It's always guaranteed to grow and get better. We get to see how the technology is changing."

Stapleton also values his apprenticeship. "Whatever class I'm in, my team leader here at the dealership will try to direct me to do that kind of job, so I can get the theoretical part and apply it to a technical part. I have a team leader who tells me, 'Okay, this is what I want you to do here and I'll be over here doing this. I know you can handle it, so if you have a problem, just run over and get me.'"

If Stapleton could talk to those considering a career in automotive technology, he would tell them, "Start as early as you can. Get experience. The more you're around cars, the more you'll understand how everything works. I wish I had done that more when I was in high school, just submerged myself into it, doing whatever I could, working at a parts store, anything, because every little bit will help you. Go to a school. Get that associate degree. If you have the degree, it opens up so many more doors."

Conclusion

Instructors are dedicated to their students. They commit long hours to their schools and their students. Sometimes they are task masters; sometimes they are counselors and surrogate parents. But at all times, they strive to graduate students who love the automotive industry and who will enter into careers that will both challenge and reward them. Most came into the automotive technology field decades before the age of computers and the rise of electronics in cars. They have adapted to the rapid changes in the field and foresee even more changes in the future.

AUT Instructor Profile: Michael Shoebroek

By 1995, Michael Shoebroek, Automotive Technology Department Chair at Austin Community College, was a working tech. "I knew I didn't want to be chained to a desk. I've always liked to work with my hands." When Shoebroek first started teaching, he didn't have a curriculum or desks or chairs, just pallets of special tools from Chrysler, still in their wrapping. His first summer, he spent 140 hours submerged in Chrysler training.

Technology constantly advances in the automotive technology field. Carburetors are gone. Computers are in -- many of them in one car. Shoebroek says, "Technology changes. Learning never ends. The method or delivery of the instruction hasn't really changed. We need to have examples of this technology to show the students. ACC is going to purchase a vehicle, a Toyota Prius, so we can teach the hybrid technology."

For Shoebroek, teaching is more hands-on than cerebral. He believes students need to learn with their hands as much as their ears. "The students most interested are the most successful. And that would be true no matter what the subject matter. They come to class on time. They're interested in what the instructor has to say. They pay attention. Sometimes, you the teacher has to adapt to the students' learning style. The students that come to us are the ones that learn by using their hands. Our processes are geared toward that. What I mean by that is, yes, we use the Socratic method -- we talk about what we're doing, observation, PowerPoints -- but our lectures are minimal compared to our shop time. One-quarter to one-third of the time in the classroom is spent talking about it, then we spend the rest of the time out in the shop."

He encourages his students to maintain and add to a portfolio -- ASE certificates, class certificates as well as things outside of the classroom that show character and dedication, like Eagle Scout awards, volunteer work or other things done out in the public. When a graduating tech comes into a job interview, his portfolio could open the door with that shop, get him chosen over someone without a portfolio, or position him for a higher starting salary.

"I enjoy teaching when I see the lights come on in students and it's clear they've 'got' it. That's exciting for me. Or you take students starting a beginning class, where they don't know much of anything, and by the end of the semester, they can pull in a vehicle, diagnose it, tell you what's wrong with it, and then go out and fix it. That gives you affirmation you're doing the right thing, you've done your job -- and that's exciting."

Chapter 3: Additional Automotive Technician Information & Resources

Although techs these days do sometimes get grease under their nails, they're more likely to spend time using computers to diagnose. Cecil Hebert, Service Manager with Champion Toyota in Austin, Texas, says, "It's not so much the old grunt work that it used to be. Some people have the idea that shops are dark, dingy, dirty places to work. It's not really that way today. We hardly ever get our hands dirty anymore. Today's techs have to be computer savvy or at least embrace a technical attitude."

Most new and working techs will tell you they love what they do. Mike Stapleton, student and working tech at Westside Lexus in Houston, Texas, says, "After graduation, if it was up to me, I'd stay right here at this dealership. I like it a lot. It's very nice, organized, technical. Everybody's serious. Everything's organized. There's procedure for it. That's just the way I'm set up."

Ray Hitchcock, Master Technician with America's Service Station in Bee Cave, Texas, prefers independents over dealerships. "I like the company I'm with now. I like the owner. I'm not going to lie; I'm making a good career here. If you find the place you like, stick with that place. I think this is a great field and you'll have a good life. There's always that one shop you're going to go to that's just going to be the one for you."

AUT Higher Education Programs in the United States

Alabama

G.C. Wallace Community College
Dothan, AL
Tom Sheff
http://wallace.edu/
(334) 556-2253

J.F. Drake State Technical College
Huntsville, AL
Scotty McLaughlin
http://www.dstc.cc.al.us/
(256) 551-3143

L.B.W. Community College - MacArthur Campus
Opp, AL
Richard McCuistian
http://www.lbwcc.edu/
(334) 493-3573

Lawrence County Center of Technology
Moulton, AL
Jerry Ellis
(256) 905-2425

Lawson State Community College
Bessemer, AL
Tom Berryman
tberryman@lawsonstate.edu
http://www.lawsonstate.edu/
(205) 929-3483

Selma High School
Selma, AL
Timothy Strong
(334) 874-1689

Alaska

Alaska Vocational Technical Center
Seward, AK
Kenny Laird
http://www.avtec.edu/
(907) 862-1683

University of Alaska
Anchorage, AK
Kelly Smith
http://www.uaa.alaska.edu/
(907) 786-1463

University of Alaska Southeast
Juneau, AK
Tony Martin
http://www.uas.alaska.edu/automotive/
(907) 796-6126

Arizona

Arizona Western College
Yuma, AZ
Larry Stanley
http://www.azwestern.edu/
(928) 344-7569

GateWay Community College
Phoenix, AZ
Thomas Goetz
http://about.gatewaycc.edu/
(602) 286-8629

Glendale Community College
Glendale, AZ
Jay Covey
http://www.gc.maricopa.edu/
(623) 845-3950

Mesa Community College
Mesa, AZ
http://www.mc.maricopa.edu/
Joe Rauscher
(480) 461-7136

Northland Pioneer College
Holbrook, AZ
Thomas Munde
http://www.npc.edu/
(928) 532-6839

Pima Community College
Tucson, AZ
Kelly Brumbaugh
http://www.pima.edu/
(520) 206-7194

Universal Technical Institute
Avondale, AZ
Ken Zwilling
http://www.uti.edu/
(623) 445-9446

Arkansas

Arkansas State University Tech Center
Marked Tree, AR
David Ashlock
http://www.asutc.org/
(870) 358-2117

Arkansas State University - Searcy
Searcy, AR
Curtis Traylor
http://www.asub.edu/
(501) 405-4024

Arkansas Tech University Ozark Campus
Ozark, AR
Kenneth Warden
(501) 667-2117

Black River Technical College
Pocahontas, AR
Travis DeClerk
http://www.blackrivertech.org/
(870) 248-4000

Cossatot Community College of the
University of Arkansas
DeQueen, AR
Mark Kutak
http://www.cccua.edu/
(870) 584-4471

Crowley's Ridge Technical Institute
Forrest City, AR
James Laws
http://www.crti.tec.ar.us/
(870) 633-5411

National Park Community College
Hot Springs, AR
Tim Hutchins
http://www.npcc.edu/
(501) 760-4309

Northwest Technical Institute
Springdale, AR
George Burch
http://www.nti.tec.ar.us/
(479) 751-8824

Ozarka Technical College
Melbourne, AR
Larry Wilkes
http://www.ozarka.edu/
(870) 368-7371

U.A.M. College of Technology - McGehee
McGehee, AR
Vickey Haycox
http://www.uamont.edu/

California

Abram Friedman Occupational Center
Los Angeles, CA
Howard Jones
http://afoc.adultinstruction.org/
(213) 765-2400

American River College
Sacramento, CA
Benjamin French
http://www.arc.losrios.edu/
(916) 484-8671

Bakersfield College
Bakersfield, CA
Carl Jones
http://www.bakersfieldcollege.edu/
(661) 395-4574

Butte College
Oroville, CA
Thomas Baird
http://www.butte.edu/
(530) 895-2448

Cerritos Community College
Norwalk, CA
Steve Berklite
http://www.cerritos.edu/
(562) 860-2451

Chabot College
Hayward, CA
Thomas Clark
http://www.chabotcollege.edu/
(510) 723-6652

Citrus Community College
Glendora, CA
Dennis Korn
http://www.citrus.cc.ca.us/
(626) 914-8738

City College of San Francisco
San Francisco, CA
Ben Macri
http://www.ccsf.edu/
(415) 550-4442

College of Alameda
Alameda, CA
Richard Greenspan
http://alameda.peralta.edu/
(510) 748-2309

College of the Redwoods
Eureka, CA
Michael Richards
http://www.redwoods.edu/
(707) 476-4345

Columbia College
Sonora, CA
Erik Andal
http://columbia.yosemite.cc.ca.us/
(209) 588-5200

Cuesta College
San Luis Obispo, CA
John Stokes
http://www.cuesta.edu/
(805) 546-3100

Cuyamaca College
El Cajon, CA
Jim Custeau
http://www.cuyamaca.edu/
(619) 660-4334

Cypress College
Cypress, CA
Chuck Sherard
http://cypresscollege.edu/
(714) 484-7234

De Anza College
Cupertino, CA
Michael Brandt
http://www.autotech.deanza.fhda.edu/
(408) 864-8527

East Los Angeles College
Monterey Park, CA
Adrian Banuelos
http://www.elac.edu/
(323) 265-8726

Evergreen Valley College
San Jose, CA
David Ames
http://www.evc.edu/
(408) 274-7900

Fresno City College
Fresno, CA
Martin Kamimoto
http://www.fresnocitycollege.edu/
(559) 442-4600

Fullerton College
Fullerton, CA
Robert Berryhill
http://www.fullcoll.edu/
(714) 992-7246

Long Beach City College
Long Beach, CA
Cal Macy
http://www.lbcc.edu/

Merced College
Merced, CA
Aaron Gregory
http://www.mccd.edu/
(209) 386-6677

Mt. San Jacinto Community College
San Jacinto, CA
Oudyalack Rampersad
http://www.msjc.edu/
(951) 487-6752

Oxnard College
Oxnard, CA
Andrew Cawelti
http://www.oxnardcollege.edu/
(805) 986-5800

Pasadena City College
Pasadena, CA
Jason Norris
http://www.pasadena.edu/
(626) 585-7685

Pierce College
Woodland Hills, CA
Thomas Rosdahl
http://www.piercecollege.edu/
(818) 710-2975

Rio Hondo College
Whittier, CA
Mike Slavich
http://www.riohondo.edu/tech/auto/
(562) 692-0921

Riverside Community College
Riverside, CA
Paul O'Connell
http://www.rcc.edu/
(951) 222-8348

San Diego Miramar College
San Diego, CA
Greg Newhouse
http://www.sdmiramar.edu/
(619) 388-7673

San Joaquin Delta College
Stockton, CA
Alberto Luna
http://www.deltacollege.edu/
(209) 954-5233

Santa Barbara City College
Santa Barbara, CA
David Brainerd
http://www.sbcc.edu/automotive/
(805) 965-0581

Shasta College
Redding, CA
Raleigh Ross
http://www.shastacollege.edu/
(530) 225-4903

Skyline College
San Bruno, CA
Rick Escalambre
http://www.skylinecollege.edu/automotive/
(650) 738-4410

Universal Technical Institute
Sacramento, CA
Dave VanWingerden
http://www.uti.edu/
(704) 489-8319

Universal Technical Institute
Rancho Cucamonga, CA
Ken Zwilling
http://www.uti.edu/
(623) 445-9446

Ventura College
Ventura, CA
Alan Penuela
http://www.venturacollege.edu/
(805) 388-5480

Victor Valley Community College
Victorville, CA
John Sweet
http://www.vvc.edu/
(760) 245-4271

West Valley Occupational Center - AYES
Woodland Hills, CA
Michael McLouth
http://www.wvoc.net/
(818) 346-3540

WyoTech - Fremont Campus
Fremont, CA
Donald Moore
http://www.wyotech.edu/campus/fremont

WyoTech
Long Beach, CA
Maryam Ashtiani
http://www.wyotech.edu/campus/long_beach
(562) 437-0501

Yuba College
Marysville, CA
Mike Morse
http://www.yccd.edu/yuba/
(530) 741-6921

Colorado

Aims Community College - AYES
Greeley, CO
Mark Brothe
http://www.aims.edu/
(970) 339-6277

Arapahoe Community College - AYES
Littleton, CO
Jerry Viola
http://www.arapahoe.edu/
(303) 797-5846

Front Range Community College
Westminster, CO
Gary Cryan
http://www.frontrange.edu/
(303) 404-5381

Morgan Community College
Fort Morgan, CO
Brad Parker
http://www.morgancc.edu
(970) 542-3215

Northeastern Junior College
Sterling, CO
Kent Wright
http://www.njc.edu/autotech/home.html
(970) 521-6694

Pikes Peak Community College
Colorado Springs, CO
Larry Schneider
http://www.ppcc.cccoes.edu/
(719) 502-3142

Pueblo Community College - AYES
Pueblo, CO
Robert Maez
http://www.pueblocc.edu/
(719) 545-3354

San Juan Basin Technical College
Mancos, CO
Barry Hicks
http://www.sanjuanbasintechschool.org
(970) 565-8457

Western Colorado Community College
Grand Junction, CO
Gary Looft
http://www.mesastate.edu/wccc/
(970) 255-2612

Connecticut

Baran Institute of Technology - Windsor
East Windsor, CT
Ron Zaccardi
http://www.baraninstitute.com/
(860) 627-4300

Gateway Community Technical College
North Haven, CT
Wayne Demske
http://www.gwcc.commnet.edu/
(203) 285-2334

Porter and Chester Institute
Branford, CT
Peter Leone
http://www.porterchester.com/
(203) 315-1060

Delaware

Delaware Technical & Community College
Georgetown, DE
Samuel Brittingham
http://www.dtcc.edu/
(302) 855-5920

District of Columbia

Montgomery College - Washington Area NADA
Washington, DC
Steve Boden
http://www.montgomerycollege.edu/
(301) 602-8979

The Excel Institute
Washington, DC
Joseph McCoy
http://www.theexcelinstitute.org/
(202) 387-1550

Florida

Atlantic Technical Center
Coconut Creek, FL
Kenneth Bergmann
http://www.atlantictechcenter.com/
(754) 321-5169

Brevard Community College
Cocoa, FL
Glenn Forester
http://www.brevard.cc.fl.us/
(321) 433-7631

Brewster Tech Center
Tampa, FL
Robert Russell
http://www.brewster.edu/
(813) 276-5448

Broward Community College
Miramar, FL
Charles Woodard
http://www.broward.edu/auto/
(954) 201-8601

Charlotte Technical Center - AYES
Port Charlotte, FL
Fred Stuenkel
http://www.ccps.k12.fl.us/
(941) 255-7500

Chipola College
Marianna, FL
John Gardner
http://www.chipola.edu/
(850) 718-2306

Florida Community College - GM ASEP
Jacksonville, FL
Donnie Thompson
http://www.fccj.edu/campuses/downtown/atc/
(904) 633-8334

George Stone Technical Center
Pensacola, FL
James Nevels
http://www.escambia.k12.fl.us/schscnts/STOC/Master/Index.asp
(850) 941-6200

Indian River Community College
Fort Pierce, FL
Randall Pollmeier
http://www.ircc.edu/
(772) 462-7747

Lee County High Tech Center - AYES
Fort Myers, FL
Marc Michaud
http://www.hightechcentral.org/
(239) 334-4544

Lindsey Hopkins Technical Education Center
Miami, FL
Tom Nunn
http://lindsey.dadeschools.net/
(305) 324-6070

Lively Technical Center - AYES
Tallahassee, FL
Gregg Hoover
http://www.livelytech.com/

Mid-Florida Technical Institute
Orlando, FL
Patricia Miles
https://www.ocps.net/
(407) 251-6000

Palm Beach Community College
Lake Worth, FL
Luis Tamayo
http://www.pbcc.edu/AutoService.xml
(561) 868-3542

Pensacola Junior College
Pensacola, FL
Bob Pierce
http://www.pjc.edu/
(850) 484-1949

Santa Fe Community College
Gainesville, FL
Mario Schwarz
http://inst.sfcc.edu/~intech/auto/
(352) 395-5250

Seminole Community College
Sanford, FL
Mark Davis
http://www.scc-fl.edu/automotive/tact/
(407) 328-2412

South Florida Community College
Avon Park, FL
Daniel Keller
http://www.sfcc.cc.fl.us/
(863) 784-7144

Universal Technical Institute
Orlando, FL
Wayne Lehnert
(407) 240-2422

Georgia

Altamaha Technical College
Jessup, GA
Michael Moore
http://www.altamahatech.edu/
(912) 427-5831

Appalachian Technical College
Jasper, GA
David Green
http://www.appalachiantech.edu/
(770) 402-5936

Athens Technical College
Athens, GA
Micheal Adkins
http://www.athenstech.edu
(706) 355-5095

Augusta Technical College
Augusta, GA
Tim Lewis
http://www.augustatech.edu/
(706) 771-4110

Central Georgia Technical College
Milledgeville, GA
James Wilkes
http://www.centralgatech.edu
(478) 445-2327

Columbus Technical College
Columbus, GA
Tommy Wilson
http://www.columbustech.edu/
(706) 649-1894

Coosa Valley Technical College
Rome, GA
Rodney Parris
http://www.coosavalleytech.edu/
(706) 295-6999

Dalton State College
Dalton, GA
Milton Brown
http://www.daltonstate.edu/
(706) 272-4434

Griffin Technical College
Griffin, GA
Clifton Owen
http://www.griffintech.edu/
(770) 228-7378

Gwinnett Technical College
Lawrenceville, GA
Steve Conway
http://www.gwinnetttech.edu/
(678) 226-6259

Heart of Georgia Technical College
Dublin, GA
Brett Colston
http://www.hgtc.org/
(478) 274-7867

Moultrie Technical College
Moultrie, GA
Kenneth Tanner
http://www.moultrietech.edu/
(229) 217-4154

Okefenokee Technical College
Waycross, GA
Larry Carr
http://www.okefenokeetech.org/
(912) 287-5825

Savannah Technical College
Savannah, GA
Ben Rodriguez
http://www.savannahtech.edu/
(912) 303-1761

Southwest Georgia Technical College
Thomasville, GA
Thomas Graham
http://www.southwestgatech.edu/
(229) 225-5085

Valdosta Technical College
Valdosta, GA
Steve Bilger
http://www.valdostatech.edu/
(229) 333-2115

West Central Technical College
Carrollton, GA
Douglas Hulsey
http://www.westcentraltech.edu/
(770) 836-4707

West Georgia Technical College
LaGrange, GA
Russell Cook
http://www.westgatech.edu/
(706) 845-4323

Hawaii

Leeward Community College
Pearl City, HI
Jake Darakjian
http://www.leeward.hawaii.edu/
(808) 455-0438

Idaho

College of Southern Idaho - GM ASEP
Twin Falls, ID
Todd Schwarz
http://www.csi.edu
(208) 732-6325

Eastern Idaho Technical College
Idaho Falls, ID
Kent Berggren
http://www.eitc.edu/
(208) 524-3000

Larry Selland College of Applied Technology
Boise, ID
Steve Rayburn
http://www.selland.boisestate.edu/
(208) 426-1241

Lewis-Clark State College
Lewiston, ID
Michael Hill
http://www.lcsc.edu/
(208) 792-2302

North Idaho College
Coeur d'Alene, ID
Mike Swaim
http://www.nic.edu/
(208) 769-3461

Illinois

College of Lake County
Grayslake, IL
Lance David
http://www.clcillinois.edu/
(847) 543-2509

Harry S. Truman College
Chicago, IL
Harold Santamaria
http://www.trumancollege.cc/
(773) 907-3984

Highland Community College
Freeport, IL
James Palmer
http://www.highland.edu/
(815) 599-3554

Illinois Central College
East Peoria, IL
Roger Donovan
http://www.icc.edu/
(309) 694-5583

Illinois Valley Community College
Oglesby, IL
Art Koudelka
http://www.ivcc.edu/automotive.aspx
(815) 224-2720

John A. Logan College
Carterville, IL
Keith Kendrick
http://jalc.edu/
(618) 985-3741

Joliet Junior College
Joliet, IL
Lynn Graf
http://www.jjc.edu/new/
(815) 280-2554

Kishwaukee College
Malta, IL
Shawn Long
http://www.kishwaukeecollege.edu/

Lake Land College
Mattoon, IL
Kevin Miller
http://www.lakelandcollege.edu/
(217) 234-5286

Lewis & Clark Community College
Godfrey, IL
Ronald Tuetken
http://www.lc.edu/
(618) 468-4910

Lincoln Technical Institute
Melrose Park, IL
James Clarke
http://www.lincolnedu.com/schools/lincoln-technical-institute
(708) 344-4700

Moraine Valley Community College
Palos Hills, IL
Richard Rackow
http://www.morainevalley.edu/automotive/
(708) 974-5713

Morton College
Cicero, IL
Dave Hostert
http://www.morton.edu/
(708) 656-8000

Parkland College
Champaign, IL
Jonathan Ross
http://www.parkland.edu/
(217) 351-2209

Parkland College - Ford ASSET
Champaign, IL
Mark Fruendt
http://www.parkland.edu/est/fordasset/
(217) 373-3765

Prairie State College
Chicago Heights, IL
Tony Gumushian
http://www.prairiestate.edu/
(708) 709-3614

Rend Lake College
Ina, IL
Shannon Perkins
http://www.rlc.edu/
(618) 437-5321

Richland Community College
Decatur, IL
Curtis Happe
http://www.richland.edu/
(217) 875-7211

Rock Valley College
Rockford, IL
Dennis Palmer
http://www.rockvalleycollege.edu/
(815) 921-3007

Shawnee Community College
Ullin, IL
Clyde Shafer
http://www.shawneecc.edu/
(618) 634-3200

Southern Illinois University - Carbondale
Carbondale, IL
Sean Boyle
http://www.siucautomotive.com/
(618) 453-4024

Triton College
River Grove, IL
Mark Robinson
http://www.triton.edu/
(708) 456-0300

Universal Technical Institute
Glendale Heights, IL
Ken Zwilling
http://www.uti.edu/
(623) 445-9446

Waubonsee Community College
Sugar Grove, IL
Ken Kunz
http://www.waubonsee.edu/
(630) 466-2331

Indiana

Ivy Tech Community College - Evansville
Evansville, IN
Mark Lammers
http://www.ivytech.edu/
(812) 422-0296

Lincoln Technical Institute
Indianapolis, IN
Dale Shepperson
http://www.lincolnedu.com/campus/indianapolis-in
(317) 632-5553

Vincennes University
Vincennes, IN
Ty Freed
http://www.vinu.edu/
(812) 888-5316

Iowa

Des Moines Area Community College
Ankeny, IA
Jeff Calkin
http://www.dmacc.edu/programs/automotive/

Hawkeye Community College
Waterloo, IA
Jim Ingles
http://www.hawkeye.cc.ia.us/
(319) 296-2320

Indian Hills Community College
Ottumwa, IA
Daniel Terrian
http://www.indianhills.edu/
(641) 683-5242

Iowa Central Community College
Fort Dodge, IA
Rob Hepperle
http://www.iccc.cc.ia.us/

Iowa Lakes Community College
Emmetsburg, IA
Larry Danielson
http://www.iowalakes.edu/
(712) 852-5215

Iowa Western Community College
Council Bluffs, IA
Jerry Nissen
http://www.iwcc.edu/programs/departments/auto.asp
(712) 388-6806

Kirkwood Community College
Cedar Rapids, IA
Gary Jorgenson
http://www.kirkwood.edu/
(319) 398-5474

North Iowa Area Community College
Mason City, IA
Greg Arrowood
http://www.niacc.edu/industrial/automotive.html
(641) 422-4243

Scott Community College
Bettendorf, IA
Darrell Hanan
http://www.eicc.edu/general/scott/
(563) 441-4228

Southeastern Community College
West Burlington, IA
Laura Menke
http://www.secc.cc.ia.us/about/

Western Iowa Tech Community College
Sioux City, IA
Shane Sampson
http://www.witcc.com/
(712) 274-8733

Kansas

Barton County Community College
Great Bend, KS
Darcy Wedel
http://www.bartonccc.edu/autotechnology/
(620) 792-9336

Butler County Community College
El Dorado, KS
Mike Fatkin
http://www.butlercc.edu/
(316) 322-3350

Coffeyville Community College
Coffeyville, KS
Roy Shafer
http://www.coffeyville.edu/
(620) 252-7550

Cowley County Community College
Arkansas City, KS
Bruce Crouse
http://www.cowley.edu/
(620) 441-5219

Flint Hills Technical College
Emporia, KS
Kathy Bode
http://www.fhtc.edu/
(620) 341-2300

Garden City Community College
Garden City, KS
Robert Schreiber
(620) 276-9659

North Central Kansas Technical College
Beloit, KS
Robert Gibbens
http://www.ncktc.edu/
(785) 738-9011

Northeast Kansas Technical College
Atchison, KS
Terri Ball
http://www.nektc.net/
(913) 367-6204

Northwest Kansas Technical College
Goodland, KS
Jim Kennedy
http://www.nwktc.edu/
(785) 890-3781

Pittsburg State University
Pittsburg, KS
Perry Cummins
http://www.pittstate.edu/
(620) 235-4827

Pratt Community College
Pratt, KS
Daryl Lucas
http://www.prattcc.edu/
(620) 672-5641

Salina Area Technical School
Salina, KS
Tom Conway
http://www.salinatech.com/

Southwest Kansas Technical School
Liberal, KS
Charles Hollar
http://www.usd480.net/SWKTS/main.html
(316) 626-3819

Wichita Area Tech College
Wichita, KS
David Lake
http://www.watc.edu/

Kentucky

Ashland Community and Technical College
Ashland, KY
John Bradley
http://www.ashland.kctcs.edu/
(606) 326-2475

Big Sandy Community & Technical College - Pikeville
Campus
Pikeville, KY
Forrest Stewardson
http://www.bigsandy.kctcs.edu/
(606) 218-2084

Bluegrass Community Technical College
Lexington, KY
Steve Johnson
http://www.bluegrass.kctcs.edu
(859) 246-2400

Elizabethtown Community and Technical College
Elizabethtown, KY
Leslie Pike
http://www.elizabethtown.kctcs.edu/
(270) 706-8657

Gateway Community & Technical College
Covington, KY
Samuel Collier
http://www.gateway.kctcs.edu/
(859) 442-1146

Jefferson Community & Technical College
Louisville, KY
Russell Wolff
http://www.jefferson.kctcs.edu/

Owensboro Community & Tech College - SE Campus
Owensboro, KY
Paul Barrett
http://www.octc.kctcs.edu/
(270) 686-4461

Somerset Community College - Laurel South
London, KY
Clevern Chadwell
http://www.somerset.kctcs.edu/
(606) 877-4735

Southeast Kentucky Community College - Harlan
Campus
Harlan, KY
Ronnie Daniels
http://www.southeast.kctcs.edu/
(606) 573-1506

UAW/LETC - Advanced Auto Training Program
Morganfield, KY
Daniel Hall
http://www.uawletc.com/
(270) 389-5311

Louisiana

Carville Job Corps Academy - General Service Tech
Carville, LA
Lane Linton
http://carville.jobcorps.gov/
(225) 642-2481

Delgado Community College
New Orleans, LA
Joseph Cruthirds
http://www.dcc.edu/
(504) 671-6192

L.E. Fletcher Technical Community College
Houma, LA
William Tulak
http://www.ftcc.edu/
(985) 857-3655

LTC
Sorrento, LA
Robert Herbert
http://www.ltc.edu/ascensioncampus/
(225) 675-5398

Sowela Community Technical College
Dequincy, LA
Lewis Williams
(337) 786-7963
Lake Charles, LA
Daniel Stuber
(337) 491-2698

Maine

Central Maine Community College
Auburn, ME
Paul Gagnon
http://www.cmcc.edu/
(207) 755-5320

Northern Maine Community College
Presque Isle, ME
Brian McDougal
http://www.nmcc.edu/
(270) 768-2763

Southern Maine Community College
South Portland, ME
Richard Thomas
http://www.smccme.edu/
(207) 741-5851

Washington County Community College
Calais, ME
Ronald O'Brien
http://www.wccc.me.edu/
(207) 454-1065

Maryland

Allegany College of Maryland
Cumberland, MD
Dennis McKenzie
http://www.ac.cc.md.us/
(301) 784-5150

Community College of Baltimore County
Baltimore, MD
Terry Wolfe
http://www.ccbcmd.edu/
(410) 455-4968

Lincoln Technical Institute
Columbia, MD
Arlen Crabb
http://www.lincolnedu.com/schools/lincoln-technical institute
(410) 290-7100

Montgomery College
Rockville, MD
Albert Ennulat
http://www.montgomerycollege.edu/

Massachusetts

Benjamin Franklin Institute of Technology
Boston, MA
David Protano
http://www.bfit.edu/
(617) 423-4630

Massachusetts Bay Community College
Ashland, MA
http://www.massbay.edu/
John Gallagher
(781) 239-3045
Timothy Caley
(781) 239-3042
Howard Ferris
(781) 239-3031

Mount Wachusett Community College
Gardner, MA
Peter Kaufmann
http://mwcc.mass.edu/
(978) 630-9336

Michigan

Baker College
http://www.baker.edu/
Clinton Township, MI
Ross Oskui
(586) 790-9726
Flint, MI
Jack Larmor
(810) 766-4110
Owosso, MI
Jeff Chapko
(989) 729-3407

Bay de Noc Community College
Escanaba, MI
Mark Loman
http://www.baycollege.edu/
(906) 786-5802

Delta College
University Center, MI
Steve Rosin
http://www.delta.edu/

Ferris State University
Big Rapids, MI
Peter Alley
http://www.ferris.edu/
(231) 591-5987

Grand Rapids Community College
Grand Rapids, MI
Randy Lee
http://www.grcc.edu/?automotive
(616) 234-3825

Henry Ford Community College
Dearborn, MI
Gary Heinz
http://www.hfcc.edu/
(313) 845-6350

Jackson Community College
Jackson, MI
Leslie Coxon
http://www.jccmi.edu
(517) 796-8541

Kirtland Community College
Roscommon, MI
Richard Bonk
http://www.kirtland.edu/academic/aut.htm
(989) 275-5000

Macomb Community College
Warren, MI
Stan Urban
http://www.macomb.edu/
(586) 445-7290

Michigan Institute of Technology
Lapeer, MI
Daniel Avery
http://www.miit.us/
(810) 245-9380

Mid Michigan Community College
Harrison, MI
David Demski
http://www.midmich.edu/
(517) 386-6642

Mott Community College
Flint, MI
John Sharpe
http://www.mcc.edu/
(810) 232-7560

Wayne County Community College District
Taylor, MI
Ethel Cronk
http://www.wcccd.edu/
(734) 374-3200

Minnesota

Anoka Technical College
Anoka, MN
John Johnson
http://anokatech.edu/
(763) 576-4852

Central Lakes College
Brainerd, MN
Raymond Johnson
http://www.clc.mnscu.edu/
(218) 855-8114

Century College
White Bear Lake, MN
Bob Olson
http://www.century.edu/
(651) 779-3429

Dakota County Technical College
Rosemount, MN
Mike Opp
http://www.dctc.edu/
(651) 423-8232

Dunwoody College of Technology
Minneapolis, MN
Charles Bowen
http://www.dunwoody.edu/
(612) 381-3086

Hennepin Technical College
http://www.hennepintech.edu/
Eden Prairie, MN
Mike Roberts
(952) 995-1558
Brooklyn Park, MN
Mike Rudolph
(763) 488-2410

Hibbing Community College
Hibbing, MN
George Sletta
http://www.hibbing.edu/

Minnesota State Community & Technical College
http://www.minnesota.edu/
Moorhead, MN
Robert Schulze
(218) 299-6548
Detroit Lakes, MN
Joe Griffin
(218) 846-3790

Minnesota West Community & Technical College
Jackson, MN
Doug Kleeberger
http://www.mnwest.edu/
(507) 847-7948

Northland Community & Technical College
http://www.northlandcollege.edu/
East Grand Forks, MN
Todd Anvinson
(218) 773-4802
Thief River Falls, MN
Norman Halsa
(218) 681-0805

Pine Technical College
Pine City, MN
Jim Ascheman
http://www.pinetech.edu
(320) 629-5162

Ridgewater College - Willmar Campus
Willmar, MN
Kevin Larison
http://www.ridgewater.mnscu.edu
(320) 231-2995

Riverland Community College
Albert Lea, MN
Jason Merritt
http://www.riverland.edu/
(507) 379-3377

South Central Technical College
North Mankato, MN
Richard Stelten
http://www.southcentral.edu/
(507) 389-7232

St. Cloud Technical College
St. Cloud, MN
Chuck Rauschendorfer
http://www.sctc.edu/

Mississippi

East Mississippi Community College
Mayhew, MS
Melanie Sanders
http://www.eastms.edu/
(662) 243-1904

Hinds Community College
Raymond, MS
Steve Miller
http://www.hindscc.edu/
(601) 857-3311

Mississippi Gulf Coast Community College
http://www.mgccc.edu/
Gautier, MS
Joe Tillson
(228) 497-7892
Long Beach, MS
Cherie Labat

Northwest Mississippi Community College
Senatobia, MS
David Yount
http://www.northwestms.edu/
(662) 562-3391

Pearl River Community College
Poplarville, MS
Richard Byrd
http://www.prcc.edu/

Missouri

Grand River Technical School
Chillicothe, MO
Ken Estes
http://www.grts.org/
(660) 646-3414

Linn State Technical College
Linn, MO
Jimmy Brandon
http://www.linnstate.edu/
(573) 897-5176

Longview Community College
Lee's Summit, MO
Bill Fairbanks
http://mcckc.edu/
(816) 672-2061

Ozarks Technical Community College
Springfield, MO
Jennifer Jackson
http://www.otc.edu/
(417) 447-8108

Ranken Technical College
St. Louis, MO
Dan Kania
http://www.ranken.edu/
(314) 286-4834

State Fair Community College
Sedalia, MO
Troy Holbrook
http://www.sfccmo.edu/
(660) 596-7243

Montana

Fort Peck Community College
Poplar, MT
Steve Harada
http://www.fpcc.edu/
(406) 768-5476

Montana State University - Billings
Billings, MT
Vern Gagnon
http://www.msubillings.edu/cot/programs/
progautotech.htm
(406) 247-3043

Montana State University - Northern
Havre, MT
Kevin Johnson
http://www.msun.edu/

Montana Tech - College of Technology
Butte, MT
Don Stodden
http://www.mtech.edu/
(406) 496-3752

University of Montana - Helena College of
Technology
Helena, MT
David Jones
http://www.umhelena.edu/
(406) 444-6806

Nebraska

Central Community College
Hastings, NE
Barry Lewis
http://www.cccneb.edu/

Metropolitan Community College
Omaha, NE
Carl Fielder
http://www.mccneb.edu/
(402) 738-4035

Northeast Community College
Norfolk, NE
Cal Lamprecht
http://www.northeast.edu/
(402) 844-7685

Southeast Community College
http://www.southeast.edu/
Lincoln, NE
Ken Jefferson
(402) 437-2640
Milford, NE
Rick Morphew
(402) 761-8317

Western Nebraska Community College
Scottsbluff, NE
Willie Quindt
http://www.wncc.net/
(308) 635-6083

Nevada

College of Southern Nevada
North Las Vegas, NV
Paul Pate
http://www.csn.edu/
(702) 651-4187

Truckee Meadows Community College
Reno, NV
Scott Allen
http://www.tmcc.edu/
(775) 856-5312

New Hampshire

Great Bay Community College
Robert King
Strathan, NH
http://www.greatbay.edu/
(603) 772-1194

Lakes Region Community College
Laconia, NH
Michael Parker
http://www.lrcc.edu/
(603) 524-3207

Nashua Community College
Nashua, NH
Daniel Jones
http://www.nashuacc.edu/
(603) 882-6923

White Mountains Community College
Berlin, NH
Al Host
http://www.wmcc.edu/
(603) 752-1113

New Jersey

Brookdale Community College
Lincroft, NJ
http://www.brookdalecc.edu/
Lee Blaustein
(732) 224-2747

Burlington County Institute of Technology
Westhampton, NJ
Thomas Molnar
http://www.bcit.cc/
(609) 267-4226

Camden County College
http://www.camdencc.edu/
Blackwood, NJ
Tony Marchetti
(856) 227-7200
GM ASEP
Toyota T-TEN

Gloucester County Institute of Technology
Sewell, NJ
Jeff Silvestri
http://www.gcit.org/
(856) 468-1445

Lincoln Technical Institute
Union, NJ
Anthony Allegro
http://www.lincolnedu.com/schools/lincoln-technical-institute
(908) 964-7800

Mercer County Community College
Trenton, NJ
Fred Bassini
http://www.mccc.edu/automotive/
(609) 570-3776

New Mexico

Central New Mexico Community College
Albuquerque, NM
James Gore
http://www.cnm.edu/depts/at/
(505) 224-3741

Eastern New Mexico University
Roswell, NM
Ray Torrez
http://www.enmu.edu/
(505) 624-7115

San Juan College
Farmington, NM
Kerry Meier
http://www.sanjuancollege.edu/pages/450.asp
(505) 566-3388

New York

Alfred State College of Technology
Wellsville, NY
John Garippa
http://www.alfredstate.edu/
(607) 587-3126

Apex Technical School
New York, NY
David Coffey
http://www.apexschool.net/main.htm
(212) 620-2863

Bronx Community College of CUNY
Bronx, NY
Clement Drummond
http://www.bcc.cuny.edu/
(718) 289-5213

Columbia-Greene Community College
Hudson, NY
Robert LaPorta
http://www.sunycgcc.edu/
(518) 828-4181

Delhi College of Technology
Delhi, NY
Steve Tucker
http://www.delhi.edu/
(607) 746-4144

Erie Community College
Vehicle Technical Training Center
http://www.ecc.edu/
Orchard Park, NY
Chrysler CAP - Chris Whiteford
(716) 270-2630
Ford ASSET - Edward Szczepanski
(716) 270-2628

Hudson Valley Community College
Troy, NY
Bob Ormond
https://www.hvcc.edu/
(518) 629-7272

Monroe Community College
Rochester, NY
Robert Brown
http://www.monroecc.edu/depts/apptech/
(716) 292-3746

Morrisville State College
Morrisville, NY
Joe Kidd
http://www.morrisville.edu/
(315) 684-6222

Suffolk County Community College
Selden, NY
Joseph Imperial
http://www.sunysuffolk.edu/
(631) 451-4905

SUNY Canton College of Technology
Canton, NY
Brandon Baldwin
http://www.canton.edu/
(315) 379-3866

Western Suffolk BOCES
Northport, NY
Demetri Fileas
http://www.wsboces.org/
(631) 261-3600

North Carolina

Alamance Community College
Graham, NC
Kevin Moore
http://www.alamancecc.edu/
(336) 506-4282

Asheville-Buncombe Technical Community College
Asheville, NC
David Walker
http://abtech.edu/
(828) 254-1921

Beaufort County Community College
Washington, NC
Neil Alligood
http://www.beaufortccc.edu/
(252) 940-6247

Blue Ridge Community College
Flat Rock, NC
Jim Rhodes
http://www.blueridge.edu/

Caldwell Community College & Technical Institute
Hudson, NC
Robert Smith
http://www.cccti.edu/
(828) 726-5272

Catawba Valley Community College
Hickory, NC
Randy Caudill
http://www.cvcc.edu/
(828) 327-7000

Central Carolina Community College
Sanford, NC
Charles Mann
http://www.cccc.edu/
(919) 718-7303

Central Piedmont Community College
Charlotte, NC
Kenneth Collins
http://www.cpcc.edu/
(704) 330-6659

Craven Community College
New Bern, NC
Robert Hall
http://www.cravencc.edu/
(252) 638-7347

Davidson County Community College
Lexington, NC
Chris Murphy
http://www.davidsonccc.edu/
(336) 249-8186

Fayetteville Technical Community College
Fayetteville, NC
Brian Oldham
http://www.faytechcc.edu/
(910) 678-8260

Forsyth Technical Community College
Winston-Salem, NC
David Allgood
http://www.forsythtech.edu/
(336) 757-7279

Gaston College
Dallas, NC
Michael Cloninger
http://www.gaston.edu/
(704) 922-6388

Lenoir Community College
Kinston, NC
W. Chris Jenkins
http://www.lenoircc.edu/
(252) 527-6223

Martin Community College
Williamston, NC
Steven Denis
http://www.martin.cc.nc.us/

McDowell Technical Community College
Marion, NC
Barry Spratt
http://www.mcdowelltech.cc.nc.us/
(828) 650-0671

Pitt Community College
Winterville, NC
Norman Lilley
http://www.pittcc.edu/
(252) 493-7235

Rowan-Cabarrus Community College
Salisbury, NC
Gary Bigelow
http://www.rccc.cc.nc.us/
(704) 637-0760

Sandhills Community College
Pinehurst, NC
Alex Cameron
http://www.sandhills.edu/
(910) 695-3958

Universal Technical Institute
Mooresville, NC
Keith Pittman
http://www.uti.edu/

Vance-Granville Community College
Henderson, NC
Fred Brewer
http://www.vgcc.edu/
(252) 492-2061

Wake Technical Community College
Raleigh, NC
Kenneth Betancourt
http://www.waketech.edu/

Wayne Community College
Goldsboro, NC
Craig Foucht
http://www.waynecc.edu/

Wilkes Community College
Wilkesboro, NC
Roger Brown
http://www.wilkescc.edu/wcccms/
(336) 838-6284

North Dakota

Bismarck State College
Bismarck, ND
Dean Gunsch
http://www.bismarckstate.com/
(701) 224-5594

Lake Region State College
Devils Lake, ND
Randy Olson
http://www.lrsc.edu/
(701) 662-1558

North Dakota State College of Science
Wahpeton, ND
Dennis Miller
http://www.ndscs.edu/
(701) 671-2656

United Tribes Technical College
Bismarck, ND
Marcel Gierszewski
http://www.uttc.edu/
(701) 255-3285

Williston State College
Williston, ND
Arne Lunzman
http://www.wsc.nodak.edu/
(701) 774-4274

Ohio

Columbus State Community College
Columbus, OH
Andrew Rezin
http://www.cscc.edu/autotech/
(614) 287-5303

Cuyahoga Community College
Parma, OH
Edward Kopp
http://www.tri-c.edu/
(216) 987-5224

Mid-East Career & Technology Center - Buffalo
Campus
Senecaville, OH
Rob Guentter
http://www.adultcentereducation.org/
(740) 455-3111

Ohio Technical College
Cleveland, OH
William Woessner
http://www.ohiotechnicalcollege.com/
(216) 881-1700

Owens Community College
Toledo, OH
Richard Hausmann
https://www.owens.edu/academic_dept/
transportation/

Scarlet Oaks Career Development Center - Ford
ASSET
Cincinnati, OH
Mike Belmont
http://www.greatoaks.com/
(513) 771-8840

Sinclair Community College
Dayton, OH
Michael Garblik
http://www.sinclair.edu/
(937) 512-4502

Stark State College of Technology
North Canton, OH
Randall Bennett
http://www.starkstate.edu/
(330) 494-6170

University of Northwestern Ohio
Lima, OH
Andy O'Neal
http://www.unoh.edu/
(419) 227-2048

Washington State Community College
Marietta, OH
Robert Feathers
http://www.wscc.edu/
(740) 374-8716

Oklahoma

Oklahoma City Community College
Oklahoma City, OK
Richard Steere
http://www.occc.edu/
(405) 682-1611

Oklahoma State University
Okmulgee, OK
William Voorhees
http://www.osuit.edu/
(918) 293-5390

Oregon

Central Oregon Community College
Bend, OR
Ken Mays
http://www.cocc.edu/
(503) 383-7701

Chemeketa Community College
Salem, OR
Steve Agee
http://www.chemek.cc.or.us/
(503) 399-6521

Lane Community College
Eugene, OR
Paul Croker
http://lanecc.edu/

Linn-Benton Community College
Albany, OR
Philip Krolick
http://www.linnbenton.edu/auto/
(541) 917-4602

Mt. Hood Community College
Gresham, OR
Mark Lambrecht
http://mhcc.edu/pages/1204.asp
(503) 491-7111

Portland Community College
Portland, OR
Russell Jones
http://www.pcc.edu/
(503) 977-4173

Rogue Community College
Grants Pass, OR
Chris Simper
http://www.roguecc.edu/

Umpqua Community College
Roseburg, OR
Kevin Mathweg
http://www.umpqua.edu/
(541) 440-4652

Pennsylvania

Community College of Allegheny County
Oakdale, PA
William Main
http://www.ccac.edu/
(412) 788-7375

Community College of Philadelphia
Philadelphia, PA
Richard Saxton
http://www.ccp.edu/
(267) 299-5875

Delaware County Community College
Broomall, PA
Charlie Stevenson
http://www.dccc.edu/
(610) 328-7714

Harrisburg Area Community College
Harrisburg, PA
Wayne Musser
http://www.hacc.edu/
(717) 780-2651

Johnson College
Scranton, PA
Robert Murray
http://www.johnson.edu/
(570) 702-8975

Lehigh Career & Technical Institute
Schnecksville, PA
Gary Nothstein
http://www.lcti.org/
(610) 799-1449

Monroe Career & Technical Institute
Bartonsville, PA
Pat Moyer
http://www.monroecti.org/

Northampton County Area Community College
Bethlehem, PA
Donald Bray
http://www.northampton.edu/
(610) 861-5327

Pennsylvania College of Technology
Williamsport, PA
Dale Jaenke
http://www.pct.edu/
(570) 326-3761

Rosedale Technical Institute
Pittsburgh, PA
Alice Ursin
http://www.rosedaletech.org/
(412) 521-6200

Universal Technical Institute
Exton, PA
Robert Paganini
http://www.uti.edu/

WyoTech - Blairsville
Blairsville, PA
Roy Ramsden
http://www.wyotech.edu/

Rhode Island

Motoring Technical Training Institute
East Providence, RI
Thayer Donovan
http://www.mtti.tec.ri.us/
(401) 494-4840

New England Institute of Technology
Warwick, RI
Christopher Bannister
http://www.neit.edu/
(401) 739-5000

South Carolina

Central Carolina Tech College
Sumter, SC
William Morrow
http://www.cctech.edu/
(803) 778-6674

Florence-Darlington Technical College
Florence, SC
Karl Jennings
http://www.fdtc.edu/
(843) 661-8188

Greenville Technical College
Greenville, SC
Sumner Huckaby
http://www.gvltec.edu/
(864) 250-8451

Midlands Technical College
Columbia, SC
Carson Conner
http://www.midlandstech.edu/automotive/aWelcome.
htm
(803) 738-7632

Orangeburg Calhoun Technical College
Orangeburg, SC
Don Gaskin
http://www.octech.edu/
(803) 535-1304

Piedmont Technical College
Greenwood, SC
Mike Rodgers
http://www.ptc.edu/
(864) 941-8468

Spartanburg Community College
Spartanburg, SC
Jeff Hunt
http://www.sccsc.edu/
(864) 592-4727

Trident Technical College
North Charleston, SC
Warren Dambaugh
http://www.tridenttech.org/

York Technical College
Rock Hill, SC
Jamey Abercrombie
http://www.yorktech.com/automotive/
(803) 981-7073

South Dakota

Southeast Technical Institute
Sioux Falls, SD
Gene Heeren
http://www.southeasttech.edu/
(605) 367-4888

Western Dakota Technical School
Rapid City, SD
Kevin Madd
http://www.wdt.edu/
(605) 718-2922

Tennessee

Chattanooga State Technical Community College
Chattanooga, TN
Roy Morris
http://www.chattanoogastate.edu/Industrial_
Technology/intmain.asp
(423) 697-4779

Nashville Auto-Diesel College
Nashville, TN
Jerry Johnson
http://www.lincolnedu.com/schools/nadc
(615) 650-7990

Nashville State Technical Community College
Nashville, TN
Claude Whitaker
http://www.nscc.edu/
(615) 353-3449

Southwest Tennessee Community College
Memphis, TN
Dale Railston
http://www.southwest.tn.edu/
(901) 333-4152

Tennessee Tech Center
http://www.ttcc.edu/
(931) 484-7502

Texas

Austin Community College
Austin, TX
David Foster
http://www.austincc.edu/
(512) 223-6099

Brookhaven College
Farmers Branch, TX
Don Jones
http://www.brookhavencollege.edu/
(972) 860-4189

Capitol City Trade & Technical School
Austin, TX
Bruce Munson
http://www.capcitytradetech.com/

Del Mar College
Corpus Christi, TX
Joe Livingston
http://www.delmar.edu/

Eastfield College
Mesquite, TX
Curt Jenkins
http://www.efc.dcccd.edu/
(972) 860-7128

Houston Community College
Houston, TX
Carl Clark
http://northeast.hccs.edu/
(713) 718-8100

Kilgore College
Kilgore, TX
D'Wayne Shaw
http://www.kilgore.edu/
(903) 983-8152

Lamar State College - Port Arthur
Port Arthur, TX
J.D. Taliaferro
http://www.lamarpa.edu/
(409) 984-6422

Laredo Community College
Laredo, TX
Fortunato Aldape
http://www.laredo.edu/
(956) 721-5172

Lincoln Technical Institute
Grand Prairie, TX
Troy Mennis
http://www.lincolnedu.com/schools/lincoln-technical
institute
(972) 660-5701

Midland College
Midland, TX
Ted Sumners
http://www.midland.edu/
(432) 681-6344

San Jacinto College
Pasadena, TX
Waylan Pittman
http://www.sanjac.edu/autotech/
(281) 476-1865

South Plains College
Levelland, TX
Gary Ham
http://www.southplainscollege.edu/
(806) 894-9611

South Texas College
McAllen, TX
Robert Gonzalez
http://www.southtexascollege.edu/
(956) 872-2706

St. Philip's College
San Antonio, TX
John Eichelberger
http://www.accd.edu/
(210) 531-3575

Texas State Technical College Waco
Waco, TX
Michael Huneke
http://www.waco.tstc.edu/
(254) 867-4855

Texas State Technical College Harlingen
Harlingen, TX
Enrique Ramirez
http://harlingen.tstc.edu/
(956) 364-4661

Texas State Technical College West Texas
Sweetwater, TX
James Butler
http://www.westtexas.tstc.edu/
(325) 235-8209

Tyler Junior College
Tyler, TX
Jeff Parks
http://www.tjc.edu/
(903) 510-2153

Universal Technical Institute
Houston, TX
Ed Fletcher
http://www.uti.edu
(602) 216-7613

Western Technical College
El Paso, TX
Ernie Leyva
http://www.wtc-ep.edu/
(915) 760-8109

Utah

College of Eastern Utah
Price, UT
Stan Martineau
http://www.ceu.edu/
(435) 613-5221

Dixie State College
St. George, UT
Melvin Jensen
http://new.dixie.edu/
(435) 652-7858

Salt Lake Community College
Sandy, UT
Brett Baird
http://www.slcc.edu/
(801) 957-4140

Salt Lake/Tooele ATC
Salt Lake City, UT
Jon Longo
http://www.sltatc.org/
(801) 493-8726

Snow College
http://www.snow.edu/
Ephraim, UT
Richfield, UT
Brent Reese
(435) 893-2215

UAW-LETC
Clearfield, UT
Harvey Brenner
http://www.uawletc.com/
(801) 416-4437

Utah Valley State College
Orem, UT
Robert Campbell
http://www.uvu.edu/
(801) 863-7126

Weber State University
Ogden, UT
John Kelly
http://www.weber.edu/automotive
(801) 626-7183

Vermont

Northlands Job Corps Center
Vergennes, VT
Charles Brighenti
http://northlands.jobcorps.gov/
(802) 877-0160

Virginia

Advanced Technology Institute
Virginia Beach, VA
Cenek Picka
http://www.auto.edu/
(757) 490-1241

Blue Ridge Community College
Weyers Cave, VA
Tom Mayer
http://www.brcc.edu/auto/
(540) 234-9261

Danville Community College
Danville, VA
Bill Roche
http://www.dcc.vccs.edu/
(434) 797-8534

Germanna Community College
Locust Grove, VA
John Donnelly
http://www.germanna.edu/

Northern Virginia Community College
Manassas, VA
George Bolash
http://www.nvcc.edu/campuses-and-centers/
manassas/
(703) 257-6678
Alexandria, VA
Reginald Bennett
http://www.nvcc.edu/
(703) 845-6523

Thomas Nelson Community College
Hampton, VA
Kenneth Brumley
http://www.tncc.edu/
(757) 825-2700

Tidewater Community College
Chesapeake, VA
Walter Brueggeman
http://www.tcc.edu/
(757) 822-5196

Tidewater Tech
Norfolk, VA
http://www.tidewatertechtrades.edu/
(757) 628-3300

Washington

Bates Technical College
Tacoma, WA
Michael Kinney
http://www.bates.ctc.edu/
(253) 680-7469

Bellingham Technical College
Bellingham, WA
Dan Beeson
http://www.btc.ctc.edu/
(360) 752-8403

Clark College
Vancouver, WA
Michael Godson
http://www.clark.edu/
(360) 992-2235

Columbia Basin College
Pasco, WA
Monty Prather
http://www.columbiabasin.edu/home/index.
asp?page=760
(509) 547-0511

Lake Washington Technical College
Kirkland, WA
Nolan Koreski
http://www.lwtc.edu/

Lower Columbia College
Longview, WA
Steve Byman
http://www.lowercolumbia.edu/
(360) 442-2725

Olympic College
Bremerton, WA
Steve Quinn
http://www.olympic.edu/
(360) 475-7340

Perry Technical Institute
Yakima, WA
Joe Garcia
http://www.perrytech.edu/

Renton Technical College
Renton, WA
Gary Neill
http://www.rtc.edu/
(425) 235-5824

Shoreline Community College
Seattle, WA
Donald Schultz
http://www.shoreline.edu/auto.html
(206) 546-4573

Skagit Valley College
Mount Vernon, WA
Scott Hall
http://www.skagit.edu/
(360) 416-7600

Spokane Community College - Toyota T-TEN
Spokane, WA
Paul Overfield
http://www.scc.spokane.edu/automotive/
(509) 533-7077

Walla Walla Community College
Walla Walla, WA
James Haun
http://www.wwcc.edu/CMS/
(509) 527-4693

Wenatchee Valley College
Wenatchee, WA
Blake Murray
http://www.wvc.edu/directory/departments/autotech/
(509) 682-6631

West Virginia

James Rumsey Technical Institute
Martinsburg, WV
Rodney Strawderman
http://www.jamesrumsey.net/
(304) 754-7925

Wisconsin

Blackhawk Technical College
Janesville, WI
Michael Zawlocki
http://www.blackhawk.edu/
(608) 743-4470

Chippewa Valley Technical College
Eau Claire, WI
Brian Gerrits
http://www.cvtc.edu/programs/deptpages/
automotive/
(715) 833-6313

Fox Valley Technical College
Appleton, WI
Ken Kempfer
http://www.fvtc.edu/public/
(920) 735-5779

Gateway Technical College
Kenosha, WI
William Fell
http://www.gtc.edu/
(262) 564-3924

Lakeshore Technical College
Cleveland, WI
Ben Adams
http://www.gotoltc.edu/
(920) 693-1252

Madison Area Technical College
Madison, WI
Paul Flogel
http://matcmadison.edu/matc/offerings/programs/pd/
automotive/
(608) 246-6823

Mid-State Technical College
Wisconsin Rapids, WI
John Gavinski
http://www.mstc.edu/

Milwaukee Area Technical College
Oak Creek, WI
Joseph Spitz
http://www.matc.edu/
(414) 571-4773

Moraine Park Technical College District
Fond du Lac, WI
Raj Pathare
http://www.morainepark.edu/

Nicolet Area Technical College
Rhinelander, WI
Mark Switek
http://www.nicoletcollege.edu/

Northcentral Technical College
Wausau, WI
Matt Klug
http://www.ntc.edu/

Northeast Wisconsin Technical College
Green Bay, WI
Randall Smith
http://www.nwtc.edu/
(920) 498-5664

Southwest Wisconsin Technical College
Fennimore, WI
Dan Schildgen
http://www.swtc.edu/
(608) 822-2729

Waukesha County Technical College
Pewaukee, WI
William Rockwell
http://www.wctc.edu/
(262) 691-5514

Western Technical College
La Crosse, WI
Brian Kanable
http://www.westerntc.edu/
(608) 789-6298

Wisconsin Indianhead Technical College
Superior, WI
Todd Asanovich
http://www.witc.edu/superior/
(715) 394-6677

WITC Rice Lake
Rice Lake, WI
Jeff Wahl
http://www.witc.edu/
(715) 234-7082

Wyoming

Laramie County Community College
Cheyenne, WY
Robert LaFaso
http://www.lccc.wy.edu/
(307) 778-5222

Western Wyoming Community College
Rock Springs, WY
Ken Fitschen
http://www.wwcc.wy.edu/academics/automotive/

WyoTech
Laramie, WY
Jack Longress
(307) 755-2185

AUT Two- and Four-Year Degree Plans

Automotive Technology Associate of Applied Science Degree

Associate degrees in automotive technology are generally of two categories: a generic study plan or brand-specific studies. In a generic plan, students study automotive technology as it applies to most cars, without zeroing in on a specific brand of vehicle. Such a degree will usually cover electrical and brake systems, engine repair and performance, automatic transmissions, steering and suspension, heating and air conditioning, and manual drive train and axles. In a brand-specific program, the classes teach a particular make of vehicle. Examples of manufacturer sponsored programs include:

- Toyota Technical Education Network (T-TEN)

- Chrysler College Automotive Program (CAP)

- BMW Service Technician Education Program (STEP)

- Honda Professional Automotive Career Training (PACT)

- Mercedes-Benz Enthusiasm, Loyalty, Integrity, Talent, Excellence (ELITE)

- GM Service Technical College (STC)

Graduates of these types of programs generally expect to be employed at a dealership.

The following are examples of different programs at various colleges.

Automotive Technology Associate of Applied Science Degree at Texas State Technical College Waco

A full-time student working toward an Associate of Applied Science degree in Automotive Technology at Texas State Technical College Waco can expect to complete the degree in twenty months. The degree requires sixty-six credits, nine of which are academic courses, such as science, math or social behavior. The other fifty-seven hours are in the automotive technology department. Students learn theory as well as diagnostic procedure.

TSTC Waco offers AAS degrees in Automotive Technology and in Toyota T-TEN as well as certificates in Automotive Parts Specialist, Automotive Technology Level 2, Heavy Line Technician and Toyota Technician Level 2.

Graduates of the TSTC Waco AUT program may apply for professional certification from ASE and ATRA. Obtaining certifications is important to the career of a tech since some dealerships and companies will only hire those who hold these certifications. To pass ASE tests, techs must know more than what can be learned through books or lectures. They must have hands-on experience. To make sure students gain this necessary experience, TSTC classes consist of both classroom time and labs. Approximately twenty to thirty percent of a student's time is spent in class, listening to lectures, demonstrations and power point presentations. The other seventy to eighty percent of course time is spent in labs working on vehicles and unit specific components.

An outline of the TSTC Waco AUT general program is included below:

		Texas State Technical College Waco	
Students Starting	Fall 2008	**Automotive Technology**	Total Credits: 66
First Semester			
AUMT 1305		Introduction to Automotive Technology	3
AUMT 1407		Automotive Electrical Systems	4
AUMT 1419		Automotive Engine Repair	4
ENGL 1301		Composition I	3
		Semester Totals	**14**
Second Semester			
AUMT 1445		Automotive Heating and Air Conditioning	4
AUMT 1410		Automotive Brake Systems	4
AUMT 1416		Suspension and Steering	4
HUMA 1301		Introduction to Humanities	3
		Semester Totals	**15**
Third Semester			
Varies		Science/Math Elective	3
Varies		Social Behavioral Science Elective	3
Varies		Approved Automotive Electives	4
		Semester Totals	**10**
Fourth Semester			
AUMT 2421		Automotive Electrical Lighting and Accessories	4
AUMT 2413		Manual Drive Train and Axles	4
AUMT 2417		Engine Performance Analysis I	4
Varies		General Education Elective	3
		Semester Totals	**15**

Fifth Semester			
AUMT 2425		Automatic Transmission and Transaxle	4
AUMT 2434		Engine Performance Analysis II	4
AUMT 2437		Automotive Electronics	4
		Semester Totals	**12**

Associate of Applied Science Degree at San Jacinto College, T-TEN Program

The Automotive Technology department at San Jacinto College, Pasadena, Texas, offers specialized programs in General Motors, Chrysler, Ford, Toyota, Honda and AC Delco. Each of these is a two-year program, consisting of manufacture modules, self studies, classroom time and lab exercises. Graduating students receive manufacture certifications.

The San Jacinto AUT program is probably best known for its Toyota program, ranked the top T-TEN program in the U.S. Students in the T-TEN program alternate between college classes and a work site. Students attend classes full-time for ten weeks and work at a dealership forty hours per week for six weeks. This sequence continues for the ninety-one weeks the student is in the training program. The program has been designed by Toyota Motors Inc., Gulf States Toyota and San Jacinto College. Graduates of this program usually aspire to work in a Toyota or Lexus dealership.

An outline of the Associate of Applied Science degree - Toyota Specialty at San Jacinto College is included below:

		San Jacinto College	
Students Starting	Fall 2008	Associate of Applied Science Technology	Total Credits: 66
First Semester			
AUMT 1405		Introduction to Automotive Technology	4
AUMT 1407		Automotive Electrical Systems	4
AUMT 1419		Automotive Engine Repair	4
TMTH 1313		Technical Mathematics	3
PHED		Activity	1
		Semester Totals	**16**
Second Semester		**(Spring)**	
AUMT 2321		Electrical Lighting and Accessories	3
AUMT 2417		Engine Performance Analysis I	4
ENGL 1301		Composition I	3
SPCH 1311		Speech	3
PHED		Activity	1
		Semester Totals	**14**
Third Semester		**(Summer)**	
AUMT 1171		Pre-Delivery	1
AUMT 1316		Suspension and Steering	3
AUMT 1345		Automotive Heating and Air Conditioning	4
		Semester Totals	**8**
Fourth Semester		**(Fall)**	
AUMT 1310		Automotive Brake Systems	4
AUMT 2425		Automatic Transmission & Transaxle	4
AUMT 1381		Cooperative Education/Auto/Automotive Mechanic	2
ENGL 2311		Technical Report Writing	3
SOCI 1301		Introduction to Sociology	3
		Semester Totals	**16**

Fifth Semester		(Spring)	
AUMT 2425		Manual Drive Train and Axles	3
AUMT 2434		Engine Performance Analysis II	3
AUMT 2437		Cooperative Education/Auto/Automotive Mechanic	3
Varies		Humanities or Fine Arts	3
		Semester Totals	**12**

Associate of Applied Science Degree, Tech Prep, at Austin Community College

The Automotive Technology program at Austin Community College (Austin, Texas) offers NATEF certified automotive technician training. ACC also offers an associate degree in Automotive Technology and certificates in:

- Automotive Technology Enhanced Skills

- Automotive Technician

- Automotive Drive Train Specialist

- Automotive Engine Performance Specialist

- Motorcycle Repair, Small Engine Repair

- Marine Engine Repair

- Automotive Brake and Suspension

- Automotive Heating & Air Conditioning

An outline of the Austin Community College Associate of Applied Science Degree, Automotive Technology, is included below:

		Austin Community College	
Students Starting	Fall 2008	Automotive Technology	Total Credits: 66
First Semester			
COSC 1301		Personal Computing	3
AUMT 1405		Introduction to Automotive Technology	4
AUMT 1407		Automotive Electrical Systems	4
AUMT 1419		Automotive Engine Repair	4
SPCH 1311		Introduction to Speech Communication	3
		Semester Totals	**18**
Second Semester			
ENGL 1301		English Composition I	3
AUMT 2417		Automotive Engine Performance Analysis I	4
AUMT 2425		Automotive Automatic Transmission and Transaxle	4
AUMT 1445		Automotive Heating and Air Conditioning	4
		Semester Totals	**15**
Third Semester			
AUMT 2437		Automotive Electronics	4
AUMT 2434		Automotive Engine Performance Analysis II	4
AUMT 1410		Automotive Brake Systems	4
MATH 1332		College Mathematics	3
Varies		Social and Behavioral Science	3
		Semester Totals	**18**
Fourth Semester			
AUMT 2413		Automotive Drive Train and Axles	4
AUMT 1416		Automotive Suspension and Steering Systems	4
AUMT 2489		Internship - Automobile/Automotive Mechanics Technology/Technician	4
Varies		Humanities/Fine Arts	3
		Semester Totals	**15**

Ford Maintenance & Light Repair Certificate at Texas State Technical College Harlingen

In addition to an Associate of Applied Science degree in Automotive Technology, TSTC Harlingen offers a twelve-month certificate program in Ford Maintenance & Light Repair, as well as certificates in Automotive Mechanic and Automotive Technician. In the Ford program, students learn the skills required to perform regular maintenance, light repairs and parts installation on all types of Ford, Lincoln and Mercury automobiles and light trucks. Successful students in this program will achieve Ford Motor Company and Light Repair certification, which includes:

- electrical systems

- brakes

- climate control

- steering and suspension alignment

This program was initiated by Ford Motor Company and its dealers to address the national shortage of trained dealer technicians industry-wide. Dealers in partnership with this program offer co-op opportunities and full-time employment opportunities upon completion.

An outline of the Ford Maintenance & Light Repair Certificate from TSTC Harlingen is included below:

		Texas State Technical College Harlingen	
Students Starting	Fall 2008	Certificate of Completion	Total Credits: 31
First Semester			
AUMT 1407		Automotive Electrical Systems	4
AUMT 1445		Automotive Heating & Air Conditioning	4
PSYT 1313		Frame Works for Learning: Psychology of Personal Adjustment	3
		Semester Totals	**11**
Second Semester			
AUMT 1410		Automotive Brake Systems	4
AUMT 1416		Automotive Suspension & Steering Systems	4
SPCR 1301		Communications for the Trades	3
TECM 1301		Industrial Mathematics	3
		Semester Totals	**14**
Third Semester			
AUMT 2680		Coop: Automobile/Automotive Mechanics Technology/Technician	6
		Semester Totals	**6**

Automotive Technology Bachelor of Applied Arts and Sciences Degree

In general, a student working toward a four-year baccalaureate degree is aiming to work in service management or in a management position at a dealership or large automotive company. He may go directly into a four-year plan, or he might get his associate degree before going for the bachelor's degree.

The advantage of going the associate-then-bachelor's degree plan is that a student can get a good portion of his automotive technology courses out of the way at what is usually a lower rate per class hour, then articulate those hours into the four-year school. Before taking this route, the student should either check with the two-year school to see what four-year colleges accept their hours or check with the four-year school he or she hopes to attend to see what schools can articulate hours into their requirements. Transfer of credits and other details would be made on an individual basis.

Four-Year Bachelor Degrees that Articulate Hours from TSTC Waco Automotive Technology Program

The following programs articulating TSTC Waco hours are currently pending approval.

Midwestern State University Bachelor of Applied Arts and Sciences Degree

Required Completed Courses (123-126 total hours):

- Occupational Specialty (36 hours)

- Computer Science (3 hours)

- Academic Foundations/Basic Core (48 - 51 hours)

- Professional Development (36 hours)

Conditions:

- Must take 31 hours from MWSU

- Limit 69 hours from TSTC

- Take writing proficiency exam between 60 - 90 hours

Apply for graduation two semesters prior to anticipated graduation date. Students should have no more than fifteen business hours from MSU or thirty total business hours.

Sam Houston State University Bachelor of Applied Arts and Sciences Degree

Required Completed Courses (128 total hours) with an Academic Core (47 hours).

Conditions:

- A student must have completed and received an AAS degree in a technical area and at least thirty-six hours of coursework must be in the technical area. Student must complete six hours of internship experience. If an internship experience was required for AAS degree, this may be waived.

- A minor of at least eighteen hours is required.

- Electives are selected as needed to meet

the university requirement of at least forty-two hours of advanced electives and to reach 128 hours total.

- Students must also complete forty-two advanced hours and 128 hours total.

Tarleton State University Bachelor of Applied Arts and Sciences Degree

Required Completed Courses (118 total hours):

- Academic Core taken at TSTC (13 hours)

- Academic Core taken at McLennan Community College (13 hours)

- Academic Core and Math taken at McLennan Community College or TSTC (17 hours)

- Occupational Specialization taken at TSTC (36 hours)

- Engineering Technology Curriculum taken at Tarleton State University (39 hours)

Texas Tech University Bachelor of Science in Mechanical Engineering (BSME) Degree, Five- Year Plan

Required Completed Courses (156 total hours):

- Academic Core taken at TSTC to satisfy AAS degree requirements (72 hours)

- Academic Core taken at TSTC as part of BSME degree requirements (14 hours)

Academic Core taken at TTU that complete BSME degree requirements (95 hours)

Note: Some courses are dual credit courses.

Conclusion

While it is possible to take automotive technology classes in high school, most shops and dealerships today are looking for techs with a post-secondary education. The Associate of Applied Science degree, either in a generic field of study or sponsored by a manufacturer, is most sought after by employers.

If a tech wants to go into management at a dealership or large shop, then a four-year Bachelor of Science degree is recommended.

There is a wide spectrum of courses of study to choose from and many different schools who offer the AAS in Automotive Technology. Each student needs to consider location of the school, degrees offered, courses of study, cost of courses, housing and tools, financial assistance, personal comfort fit with the school and instructors, and whether courses taken at a two-year school will articulate to a four-year college or university.

AUT Online Resources

Automotive Career Information Sites

Automotive Careers Today
http://www.autocareerstoday.net/

Automotive Retailing Today
http://www.autoretailing.org/

Automotive Service Technician Career Highlights
http://www.elearningyellowpages.com/Career
Training/AutomotiveServiceTechnicianCareer
Highlights-a2.html

Bureau of Labor Statistics: Occupational Outlook
Handbook, 2008-2009 Edition
http://www.bls.gov/oco/ocos181.htm

eLearning Yellow Pages
http://www.elearningyellowpages.com/

National Automotive Technicians Education
Foundation
http://natef.org/

National Institute for Automotive Service Excellence
(ASE)
http://asecert.org/

Occupational Employment Statistics
http://www.bls.gov/OES/

O*NET OnLine
http://online.onetcenter.org/link/details/49-3023.01

AUT Industry Publications

AutoInc.
http://www.autoinc.org/

Automotive Industries
http://www.ai-online.com/

Automotive News
http://www.autonews.com/

AutoWeek Magazine
http://www.autoweek.com/

Car Audio and Electronics
http://www.caraudiomag.com/

Car and Driver
http://www.caranddriver.com/

International Journal of Automotive Technology and
Management
http://www.inderscience.com/browse/index.
php?journalCODE=ijatm

Kit Car Magazine
http://www.kitcarmagazine.com/

Modern Machine Shop
http://www.mmsonline.com/articles/

Motor Trend Magazine
http://www.motortrend.com/

Popular Mechanics
http://www.popularmechanics.com/

Popular Science
http://www.popsci.com/

The Truth About Cars
http://www.thetruthaboutcars.com/

Top Gear Magazine
http://www.topgear.com/us/

Manufacturers/Suppliers of Hand Tools

AAMP of America
http://www.aampofamerica.com/

Air Turbine Tools
http://www.airturbinetools.com/

AmPro North America
http://www.ampro-usa.com/

API (Automated Products International)
http://www.apiclamps.com/

Bad Dog Tools
http://www.baddogtools.com/

BrakeQuip
http://www.brakequip.com/

California Torque Products
http://www.caltorque.com/

Chassis Shop Performance Products
http://chassisshop.com/

Classic Tube
http://www.classictube.com/

Competition Engineering
http://www.competitionengineering.com/

Craftsman
http://www.sears.com/

CV Products
http://www.cvproducts.com/

GearWrench
http://www.gearwrench.com/

Dill Air Controls
http://www.dillaircontrols.com/

Dyna Plug
http://www.dynaplug.com/

Elden's Tool and Design
http://www.wrenchextender.com/

Enkay Products
http://www.enkayproducts.com/

Franklin Tool Company
http://www.franklintool.com/

Industro
http://www.industroinc.com/

Jancy Engineering
http://www.jancy.com/

Made 4 You Products
http://www.made4uproducts.com/

Manley Performance Products
http://www.manleyperformance.com/

Moroso Performance Products
http://www.moroso.com/

Motive Products
http://www.motiveproducts.com/

Powerhouse Products
http://www.powerhouseproducts.com/

Proform Co.
http://www.proformparts.com/

Sarveshwari Engineers
http://www.sarveshwari.com/

Sequoia Tools
http://www.sequoia-us.com/

SK Handtools
http://www.skhandtool.com/

Spec Tools
http://www.spectools.com/indexus.html.htm

Sunex Tools
http://www.sunextools.com/

TCS Products
http://www.tcsproducts.com/

Time Shaver Tools
http://www.timeshavertools.com/

Totally Stainless
http://www.totallystainless.com/

Schools & Financial Aid

Accrediting Commission of Career Schools and
Colleges of Technology
http://www.accsct.org/

Austin Community College
http://www.austincc.edu/autotech/

Automotive Technology Financial Aid
http://www.topautomotivecolleges.com/automotive-
technology-financial-aid.html

Campus Explorer
http://www.campusexplorer.com/colleges/major/
0CA5F838/Mechanic-Repair-Trades/F2A5AE66/
Automobile-Automotive-Mechanics-Technology-
Technician/

NATEF Certified Programs in the U.S.
http://www.natef.org/certified00.cfm

Pell Grants
http://www.ed.gov/programs/fpg/

San Jacinto College
http://www.sanjac.edu/autotech/content/auto/auto.
shtml

St. Phillip's College
http://www.accd.edu/spc

Student Aid on the Web
http://studentaid.ed.gov/PORTALSWebApp/students/english/index.jsp

Texas State Technical College Harlingen
http://www.harlingen.tstc.edu/

Texas State Technical College Waco
http://www.waco.tstc.edu/aut/

Unions

International Association of Machinists and
Aerospace Workers
http://www.goiam.org/

United Auto Workers
http://www.uaw.org/

Additional Automotive Resources

Accrediting Commission of Career Schools and
Colleges of Technology
http://www.accsct.org

Automotive Oil Change Association
http://www.aoca.org/

Automotive Service Association
http://www.asashop.org/

Automotive Service Excellence
http://www.asecert.org/

Automatic Transmission Rebuilders Association
http://www.atra.com/

Automotive Undercar Trade Organization
http://www.undercar.org/

Automotive Youth Educational Systems
http://www.ayes.org

Bureau of Labor Statistics
http://www.bls.gov/oco/ocos181.htm

Equipment and Tool Institute
http://www.etools.org/

Hand Tools Institute
http://www.hti.org/

International Automotive Technicians' Network
http://www.iatn.net/

Mechanic's Education Association
http://www.meatraining.com/

National Automotive Dealers Association
http://www.nada.org/

National Automotive Technicians Education
Foundation
http://www.natef.org/

North American Council of Automotive Teachers
http://www.nacat.com/

Society of Automotive Engineers
http://www.sae.org/

Specialty Equipment Market Association
http://www.sema.org/

Service Specialists Association
http://www.truckservice.org/

Service Station Dealers of America
http://www.ssda-at.org/

Transmission Rebuilders Network International
http://www.transbuilder.com/

Used Oil Management Association
http://www.uoma.com/

INDEX

About the Author

Helen Ginger

Helen Ginger began writing when she was in grade school. After receiving her master's degree from Southwest Texas State University, she taught at San Antonio College and Incarnate Word College. She served as the Executive Director of the Writers' League of Texas and is an owner-partner in Legends In Our Own

Minds®. Helen's e-newsletter, Doing It Write, goes out to readers on every continent except the Antarctic, but she's looking for someone there too. When not writing, she edits fellow authors' books.

When asked to write *Automotive Technicians*, Helen hesitated. After all, she'd somehow gotten through life without ever having to change a tire. She wrote the book for those, like her, who want to learn about this career. She met the most interesting people: students who enjoy working on cars, teachers dedicated to their students, employers with years of experience who think there's no better profession, and working techs who love what they do and do what they do with amazing skill. Those are the people you meet in this book and in automotive shops everywhere.

TSTC Publishing

Established in 2004, TSTC Publishing is a provider of high-end technical instructional materials and related information to institutions of higher education and private industry. "High end" refers simultaneously to the information delivered, the various delivery formats of that information and the marketing of materials produced. More information about the products and services offered by TSTC Publishing may be found at its Web site: http://publishing.tstc.edu/.

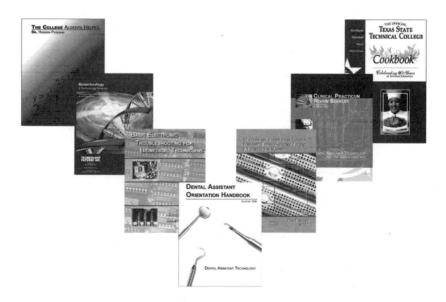

Notes

Notes

Notes

Notes

Notes